Casemate Short History

SHARPSHOOTERS

MARKSMEN THROUGH THE AGES

Gary Yee

CASEMATE

Oxford & Philadelphia

Published in Great Britain and
the United States of America in 2017 by
CASEMATE PUBLISHERS
The Old Music Hall, 106–108 Cowley Road, Oxford OX4 1JE, UK and
1950 Lawrence Road, Havertown, PA 19083, USA

© Casemate Publishers 2017

Paperback Edition: ISBN 978-1-61200-486-0
Digital Edition: ISBN 978-1-61200-487-7

A CIP record for this book is available from the British Library

Printed in the Czech Republic by FINIDR, s.r.o.

For a complete list of Casemate titles, please contact:

CASEMATE PUBLISHERS (UK)
Telephone (01865) 241249
Email: casemate-uk@casematepublishers.co.uk
www.casematepublishers.co.uk

CASEMATE PUBLISHERS (US)
Telephone (610) 853-9131
Fax (610) 853-9146
Email: casemate@casematepublishers.com
www.casematepublishers.com

CONTENTS

This book is dedicated to my mother.

INTRODUCTION

THE STORY OF MARKSMANSHIP PREDATES WRITTEN history and Homer's *Odyssey* recounts Odysseus shooting an arrow through twelve ax heads to win back Penelope's hand. Centuries later the crossbow began supplanting the bow and in 1382 a Moscow cloth maker used a crossbow to slay a Tartar commander at 650 paces. Firearms gradually replaced stringed weapons and Hungarian borderers ambushed the Ottomans with them from concealment in around 1522. In 1565 the Ottomans applied their experience by sending out their matchlock-armed soldiers at Fort St. Elmo to hide in the bushes and pick off unwary Christians.

Initially firearms progress was slow and the 1466 Swiss shooting matches for matchlock firearms were held at 100 paces. Six years later, with the introduction of rifling—spiral grooves cut inside the barrel that imparted a spin to the ball that made it fly straighter for a longer distance—the distance for the matches was 230 paces. By the 16th century matches were commonly held at 250–280 paces.

Despite the rifle's superior accuracy, the smoothbore musket remained the preferred infantry arm. Volume of fire followed up with a bayonet charge decided battles, not accuracy. A skilled musketman, firing an undersized ball, quick to load, was expected to fire five times a minute. In contrast the rifle fired a tight-fitting ball that could take several minutes to load and since rifles weren't adapted to accept a bayonet, a rifleman with an empty rifle was defenseless. After a few shots, the rifle barrel fouled, making reloading more difficult, reducing the rate of fire further as the rifleman struggled to reload. Rifles then were limited as an auxiliary arm and remained largely in the hands of specialized troops. From a cost perspective, rifles were also more expensive and timely to produce. Rifling a barrel required a day's labor.

Starting with the Thirty Years' War (1618–48), rifles slowly gained acceptance when the Landgrave of Hesse armed three companies of his green-clad chasseurs with rifles. They served as scouts and guides who also harassed the enemy. Other states that issued a limited number of rifles included Bavaria (1645), Prussia (1674), and Sweden (1691). It is unknown when the Holy Roman Empire issued rifles, but rifles were in the hands of Tyrolese civilians and *grenzers* (border dwellers) of the Empire. In the early 18th century the Norwegian ski *jägers* were issued rifles.

As rifles gained acceptance, there arose a greater understanding of their potential. In 1808, writing under the pseudonym of "A Corporal of Riflemen," Captain Henry Beaufoy prophetically penned:

> When opposed to riflemen, it is the bravest who fall, for it is the bravest who expose themselves most, and thus become most conspicuous. The Officers of our own army in Holland obtained this experience, and in several instances found it necessary to change their hats, and assimilate themselves to the private men. That powerful influence on the mind also, which prevails in a variety of ways in an army, has its full effect in that by which this species of force is employed, as well as that against which it is directed. It has been readily confessed to the writer by old soldiers, that when they understood they were opposed by riflemen, they felt a degree of terror never inspired by general action, for the idea that a rifleman always singled out an individual, who was almost certain of being killed or wounded; and this individual every man with ordinary self-love expected to be himself. How much more must this influence operate, where individual danger is incurred

in heroic actions, the success of which must be rendered almost impossible, while the individual conceives himself the particular object of perhaps numerous riflemen. Destroy the mind, and bodily strength will avail but little in that courage required in the field of battle.

Accuracy and rifles traveled an arduous road before winning widespread military acceptance. As fate would decree it, by the time the muzzle-loading rifle was universally adopted, it was rendered obsolete by the breechloader. However, muzzle-loading rifles established a legacy of marksmanship that has been relegated to the dustbin of history. Almost equally forgotten is the story of the rifleman and the sharpshooter who began a tradition maintained by their heirs, today's snipers.

c. 1470	Rifling invented.
1565	Matchlock-armed Ottomans snipe at Malta's defenders of Fort St. Elmo.
c. 1630	Flintlock mechanism is invented.
1631	Landgrave of Hessia, William V, raises *jäger* companies from his forest rangers and gamekeepers.
1645–49	Bavaria, Prussia, France, and Sweden issue limited number of rifles.
1740	Frederick the Great raises *Chaussers de Cheval* (mounted *jägers*) and later his *Chaussers de Pied* (infantry *jägers*).
1759	German *jägers* delay French advance at Minden. By the Seven Years' War's conclusion the Austro-Hungarian Empire, virtually all German states as well as Russia have *jäger* companies.
1776	David Rittenhouse makes the first American scoped rifle and installs a spring-loaded recoil pad.
1794–1803	One battalion of the Royal Americans (either the 1/60 or 4/60) was equipped with rifles. Three years later 5/60 is raised by consolidating Hompesch Chasseurs and Löwenstein's *Jägers* regiment into a rifle regiment. This is followed in 1803 by placing the newly raised Rifle Corps among the numbered regiments as the 95.
1807	Andrew Forsyth discovers fulminate of mercury.
1817	Joshua Shaw invents the percussion cap.
1836	Casimir Lefauxheux invents the metallic cartridge. It is refined in 1846 by Flobert into a rimfire cartridge, making it practical for repeater designs.
1838	The first practical breechloading rifle by William Jenks was adopted by the U.S. Navy. Prussia adopts the Dreyse needle gun in 1841.

1846   Minié gun adopted by France, ending the round ball's reign as the bullet used by rifles. To take advantage of the longer range offered by the Minié gun, the French military school at Vincennes offers marksmanship classes. Other powers follow the French example and the School of Musketry at Hythe (Kent) is opened in 1854.

1856   Scoped rifle first used in combat in India.

1861–65   Scoped rifles fielded by both sides in the American Civil War. The Confederacy though is the first nation to issue them. Both breechloaders and repeater rifles are used in combat. Mirrors first used for aiming.

1866   Austro-Prussian War. Last war in which a major power uses muzzle-loaders.

1899   Boer War. "Snipers" and "sniping" see common usage.

1908   U.S. Army adopts the telescopic sight. Some are purportedly carried by Pershing's men during the Punitive Expedition in Mexico.

1914–18   Scoped rifles are used by all major powers for sniping. Periscope rifle is invented. Postwar, sniping is promptly forgotten.

1932   Soviet Union adopts sniper rifles but this offers them no advantage in the Winter War against Finland (1939–40).

1945   First infrared sights developed in Germany and the United States.

1946   Following the end of World War II, only the British Royal Marines and the Soviet Union retain snipers and sniping.

1967   AN/PVS-1 Passive night vision sight fielded in combat in Vietnam.

1998   AN/PAS-13, thermal imaging sight for small arms issued by the American military.

NOTABLE SHARPSHOOTERS AND SNIPERS

Name	Affiliation / *War*	Score or Feat
Moses Hazen	Massachusetts Colony / *French & Indian War*	Prevented French from routing retreating British at St. Foy
Tim Murphy	USA / *American Revolution*	Shot General Fraser
Ephraim Brank	USA / *War of 1812*	Ghostly spectre who unnerved an approaching column
Elijah Kirk	USA / *War of 1812*	600-yard kill
Tom Plunkett	Great Britain / *Napoleonic Wars*	20+ kills, shooting of General Colbert
Henry Muller	King's German Legion / *Napoleonic Wars*	Threw two French columns into confusion after shooting its commanding officer.
W. A. Godfrey	Great Britain / *Crimean War*	Silenced Russian battery at 600 yards
Henry Herbert	Great Britain / *Crimean War*	1,000–1,300-yard kill
Henry Tyron	Great Britain / *Crimean War*	100+ kills
Truman Head	USA / *American Civil War*	Kills at over 500 yards, use of bushes for camouflage
William Dawson Dorris	USA / *American Civil War*	117 kills

Henry Foster	USA / *American Civil War*	Burrowed into ground and dug a loophole—first sniper hide
Jack Hinson	Confederate States / *American Civil War*	36 kills. Harassed Union shipping
Billy Dixon	USA / *World War I*	1,538-yard kill
Herbert McBride	Canada / *World War I*	100+ kills
Billy Sing	Australia / *World War I*	160 kills
Francis Pegahmahabow	Canada / *Winter War*	378 kills
Sulko Kolkka	Finland / *Winter War*	400+ kills
Simo Häyhä	Finland / *Winter War*	542 kills
Matthias Hetzenauer	Germany (Austria) / *World War II*	345 kills
Sepp Alleberger	Germany / *World War II*	257 kills
Ivan Mikhailovich Sidorenko	USSR / *World War II*	500 kills
Mikhail Ivanovich Budenov	USSR / *World War II*	437 kills
Fyodor Maveyevich Ohlopkov	USSR / *World War II*	429 kills
Fyodor Trofimovich Dyachenko	USSR / *World War II*	425 kills
Vasili Ivanovich Golosov	USSR / *World War II*	422 kills
Stepan Vassilievich Petrenko	USSR / *World War II*	422 kills
Lyudmila Pavlichenko	USSR / *World War II*	309 kills. Highest-scoring female sniper
Vassili Zaitsev	USSR / *World War II*	225+ kills
Aldebert Waldron	USA / *Vietnam*	113 kills
Chuck Mawhinney	USA / *Vietnam*	103 kills
Carlos Hathcock	USA / *Vietnam*	93 kills, one at 2,286 meters
Chris Kyle	USA / *Iraq*	160 kills
James Gilliland	USA / *Iraq*	1,250-meter kill with M-24 7.62 mm NATO rifle
Nick Ranstad	USA / *Afghanistan*	2,100-meter kill
Rob Furlong	Canada / *Afghanistan*	2,430-meter kill
Craig Harrison	UK / *Afghanistan*	2,475-meter kill

Thoughts on scores from the blackpowder era to the present

Sharpshooters of the blackpowder era were not concerned with score keeping, and belief in the Commandment against killing discouraged bragging. Robert Cooper, co-author of the Rifle Green series of books on the 95 Rifle Brigade, felt the men believed they had a job to do and they did it. When not busy fighting, they saw the human element in their foe and fraternized with them. Civil War soldiers shared this view and when not fighting, exchanged newspapers, coffee for tobacco or anything else that was available.

Crediting standard varies from nation to nation and what may be a confirmed kill for one may only be a probable by another. Another point is the Soviet propensity for propaganda and that Soviet claims *might* be inflated. During World War II the propaganda value of sniping was recognized by the Russians first and then the Germans. It was meant to inspire friendly forces and to instill fear into the enemy. Western powers were not overly interested in scores until after Charles Henderson's book, *Marine Sniper* was published. Since *Marine Sniper*, sniping has public acceptance and score keeping became fashionable. In the internet age, where it is easy to locate individuals, the World War II British practice of keeping mum has validity. Last, score should not be the sole measurement of effectiveness and who is killed or the intelligence gathered can be more important.

CHAPTER 1

EARLY FLINTLOCK ERA

1700–81

"There were but very few of their officers who were not killed or wounded."

The musket's reign

CULVERINS, MATCHLOCKS, ARQUEBUS AND MOST WHEELLOCKS and flintlocks all share in common a smoothbore barrel. While not accurate at long range, with practice they could be reasonably accurate at shorter ranges (up to 75 yards). It was a matter of whether the shooter used a tight-fitting ball, sometimes attained with a patch, a skilled eye and steady hand, and a bit of luck. In battle it was not accuracy but volume of fire that mattered and linear formations of musket-armed infantry closed within short distance of each other before halting and exchanging volleys.

How accurate were muskets? Firing from a rest at a target measuring 1.75 meters by 3 meters, Prussian tests in 1800 attained 60 percent hits at 75 meters, 40 percent at 150 meters, 25 percent at 225 meters and 20 percent at 300 meters. After conducting experiments at Chatham in 1846, Colonel MacKerlie recommended that musket fire should never commence beyond

Brown Bess musket.

150 yards and even then there would be a large proportion of misses. MacKerlie noted that at 75–100 yards every ball struck the 2-feet-wide target. In tests conducted between 1969 and 1973 using a replica Brown Bess, Lawrence Babits found he could hit a man-sized target at 75 yards distance five out of six times. Babits however did one thing that most soldiers didn't do—he practiced. Practice was believed by most colonels to be a waste of powder and shot. One should also bear in mind that tests only demonstrated the musket's potential and ignored the stress of combat that includes the return fire and confusion.

Despite the musket's limitation, some long-range hits were recorded. One exceptional hit during the English Civil War (1642–51) was Royalist John Dyott's shooting of Lord Brooke at 150 yards distance. Another was witnessed by Private Plumb Martin during the American Revolution (1765–83):

[H]ere I saw a piece of American workmanship that was, as I thought, rather remarkable. Going one evening upon a picket guard … we had to march … close upon the bank of the river. There was a small party of British upon the island in the river. One of the soldiers, however, thinking perhaps he could do more mischief by killing some of us, had posted himself on a point of rocks at the southern extremity of the island and kept firing at us as we passed along the bank. Several of his shots passed along the files, but we took little notice of him, thinking he was so far off that he could do us but little hurt and that we could do him none at all, until one of the guard asked the officer if he might discharge his piece at him. [T]he officer gave his consent. He rested his old six feet barrel across a fence and sent an express to him. The man dropped, but as we thought it was only to amuse us, we took no further notice of it but passed on. In the morning upon our return, we saw the brick coloured coat still lying in the same position we had left it in the evening before. It was a long distance to hit a single man with a musket; it was certainly over half a mile.

The distance from Manhattan Island to Blackwell (modern Roosevelt) Island is 350 yards.

The Seven Years' War

Tensions between France and England ignited in 1754 when an expedition led by a young George Washington attacked and killed a French diplomat near Fort Duquesne (Pittsburgh). Retreating to a nearby meadow, Washington built a palisade fort, Fort Necessity, and awaited the retaliatory force composed of the French and their Indian allies. Ignoring the advice of his Indian ally to ambush them while they were approaching, Washington instead chose to fight in the open and anticipated the French would do the same. Instead the French and Indians remained in the woods and picked off Washington's Virginians. They fought back the best they could but when ammunition ran low and casualties mounted, Washington had to surrender. Washington unwittingly signed surrender terms that admitted that he had assassinated the French diplomat. In the wake of these incidents,

There is a myth that the Civil War-era Sharps rifle gave rise to the word **sharpshooter**. "Sharpshooter" is the English translation of the German *scharfshützen* and its adoption in the English language predates the invention of the Sharps rifle. Use of "sharpshooter" became popularized during the Napoleonic Wars.

a world war erupted that was fought not only in North America but also in the Caribbean, Europe, and India.

To recapture Fort Duquesne, Britain dispatched General Edward Braddock along with two regiments: the 44th East Essex and 48th Northamptonshire. Totaling 1,440 officers and men, they were supported by Washington's 450 colonials. Within a short march of Fort Duquesne, Braddock's column collided with a force half their size composed of French marines, Canadians, and their Indian allies on the Monongahela River. Standing exposed in their linear formations, the British fired off volleys as the Canadians and Indians melted into the woods. Indian fighting tactics were adapted from communal hunts and this enabled them to coordinate their attacks even when multi-tribal groups fought alongside one another. Applied in warfare, they enjoyed a mobility unsurpassed by any European army. Using their field craft, they seemingly disappeared only to suddenly reappear elsewhere to pick off an opponent. After four hours of fighting and having seen many of their comrades and officers shot, panic spread among the ranks and men began to flee in terror. Those who stood their ground poured un-aimed volleys into their comrades or the air while the Indians hid behind bushes, trees, rocks or in depressions in the ground. The proud little army that had marched confidently into the wilderness suffered 46 percent casualties, with 456 killed and 421 wounded. Braddock was mortally wounded, remarking before dying, "We shall better know how to deal with them another time."

Blame can neither be placed totally on the soldiers nor Braddock since no formal training of the period could prepare them for forest warfare. The lessons were not lost and the British army began adapting itself by raising light infantry and, from among the colonists, rangers who would scout and screen the army better. Men were taught to seek cover ("Tree all") and to aim at marks. Before the war, linear formations ensured an officer of his command and control over his men and they were loath to depart from the practice. Adopting open formations was quite a novel concept. Finally a limited number of rifles were distributed.

Results were not immediate but during the landing to capture Louisbourg in 1758, the 78th Fraser Highlanders came under fire. Sergeant Thompson recalled the incident:

> During the landing at Louisberg there was a rascal of a savage on top of a high rock that kept firing at the Boats as they came within his reach, and he kill'd volunteer Fraser of our Regiment who, in order to get his shilling instead of six pence a day, was acting, like myself as a sergeant, he was a very genteel young man and was to have commison'd the first vacancy. There sat next to Fraser in the boat, a silly fellow of a Highlander, but who was a good marksman for all that, and not withstanding that there was a positive order not to fire a shot during the landing, he couldn't resist this temptation of having a slap at the Savage. So the silly fellow levels his fuzee at him and in spite of the unsteadiness of the boat, for it was blowing

---

Unlike the smoothbore barrel of a musket or today's shotguns, **rifles** have spiral grooves cut along the length of the barrel. Firing an undersized ball, muskets were quick loading and a musket-armed infantryman could get anywhere from three to five shots off a minute. Rifles, to be accurate, took a tight-fitting ball or ball with patch that was laboriously rammed down the length of the barrel. This took anywhere from a minute to several minutes to load.

American long rifle.
(West Point Collection)

---

hard at the time, 'afaith he brought him tumbling down like a sack into the water as the matter so turned out, there was not a word said about it, but had it been otherwise he would have had his back scratch'd if not something worse.

After landing, 550 of the best marksmen were drawn from the available units and organized into a provisional light infantry battalion. As sharpshooters, they suppressed the defenders during the construction of the siege works. After the siege guns were mounted in the third parallel, Louisbourg surrendered.

Sergeant Thompson survived and became part of the garrison of Quebec after its capture by General James Wolfe. In the spring of 1760, when a French force arrived to retake it, the reduced British army marched out to meet it. They were defeated and began to retreat to the safety of Quebec's walls. One French column threatened to cut off the retreat and Thompson recalls the shot that prevented it:

On the way I fell in with a Captain Moses Hazen, a Jew, who commanded a company of Rangers, and who was so badly wounded, that his servant who had to carry him away was obliged to rest him on the ground at every twenty or thirty yards, owing to the great pain he endured. This intrepid fellow observing that there was a solid column of the French coming on over the high ground and headed by an officer who was some distance in advance of the column, he ask'd his servant if his fuzee was still loaded (the Servant opens the pans, and finds that it was still prim'd). "Do you see," says Captain Hazen, "that rascal there, waving his sword to encourage those fellows to come forward?" "yes," says the Servant, "I do Sir." "Then," says the Captain again, "just place your back against mine for one moment, till I see if I can bring him down." He accordingly stretch'd himself on the ground, and resting the muzzle of his fuzee on his toes he let drive at the French officer. I was standing close behind him, and I thought it perfect madness in his attempt. However, away went the charge after him, and 'afaith down he was flat in an instant! Both the Captain and myself were watching for some minutes under an idea that "altho" he had laid down, he might take it into his head to get up again, but no, the de'il a get up and did he get, it was the best shot I ever saw, and the moment he fell, the whole column he was leading on, turn'd about and decamp'd off, leaving him to follow as well as he might! I couldn't help telling the Captain that he had made a capital shot, and I related to him the affair of the foolish fellow of our Grenadiers who shot the Savage at the landing at Louisberg, altho' the distance was great and the rolling of the boat so much against his taking a steady aim. "Oh," says Captain Hazen, "you know that a chance shot will kill the devil himself!"

Captain Hazen survived and rose to brigadier general in the Continental Army during the Revolution.

Elsewhere in Europe the German *jägers* distinguished themselves at Minden (1759). Hanoverian General von Freytag dispatched some *jäger* companies to the passes between Minden and Bückeburg to harass the French. There they killed many Frenchmen until a heavy rain put an end to the shooting. Lieutenant Colonel George Hangar tells of an incident along the road from Minden to Hesse Cassel, where the Hessian and Hanoverian *jägers* were deployed in a very thick wood:

The French were obligated to form one regiment, in their line, directly facing this wood, where the jägers were stationed. The jägers made such havoc amongst this French regiment, that the colours were at last forced to be held by serjeants, and even corporals. There were but very few of their officers who were not killed or wounded. The jägers were not above two hundred yards from them, and were flanked, both on their right and left, by strong battalions of the line. The French were at last compelled to bring up six pieces of cannon, loaded with grape, to clear the woods of jägers. I had a man in my company, in the Hessian jägers, in America, who was the son of a jäger, supposed to be one of the very best shots among those engaged at Minden. His comrades had such an opinion of his shooting, that six or seven men handed their rifles to him, as he stood behind a large tree, continually keeping them loaded for him to fire, so that he could fire several shots in one minute. When the cannon were brought up, his comrades desired him to come away;

but he said he would stay, and have one shot more; a grape-shot struck him, and killed him. The French were so incensed that day against the jägers, that a few of them which they took, wounded, in the retreat, for the German forces were beaten, they buried up to their chins in the ground, and left them to die.

While the rifle was slowly gaining acceptance as a specialized weapon to be used by light troops, the war's conclusion did not see its universal adoption. The British Army returned its rifles to storage at the war's conclusion and for the most part, forgot the lessons learned.

The American Revolution

To recoup the expenses incurred during the Seven Years' War, Parliament imposed taxes on its American colonies. Parliament reasoned that since the war had been fought on their behalf, they should share in the expense. This did not sit well with the colonists whose protestations were made on paper and later by acts of violence. In response, a large British force was landed in Boston where it was felt that the mere presence of the British Army would quiet things. However, when a British column was dispatched to seize powder and cannons stored in Concord in 1775, fighting erupted between the American militia and the British regulars and blood was spilled on both sides. The Americans swarmed the British column, attacking their flanks and the rearguard. Among the militia was one hunter:

> Through their whole retreat the British had noticed one man in particular, whom they learned especially to dread. He was an old, gray-haired hunter, named Wyman of Woburn, and he rode a fine white horse. He struck the trail as they left Concord, and would ride up within gunshot, then turning the horse throw himself off, aim his long gun resting on the saddle, and that aim was death. They would say, "Look out, there is the man on the white horse."

He followed them the whole distance, and James Russell … saw him gallop across the brook and up a hill, pursued by a party of the flank guard who kept the plains midway between Charlestown and Main street. He turned, aimed and the boy saw one of the British fall. He rode on, and soon the same gun was heard again, this time also with deadly effect.

The British reached the safety of Boston but not without first suffering 73 killed, 26 missing, and 174 wounded. The Americans suffered 49 killed, five missing and 41 wounded. Making no attempt to capture Boston by coup de main, the Americans began entrenching around it.

One of the first acts of Congress was to raise the 1st Pennsylvania from among the riflemen of Pennsylvania, Virginia, and Maryland. These men were excellent marksmen and one company, Captain Doudle's, marched from Getty's Tavern (Gettysburg) to Boston in 25 days. As with other frontiersmen, they were unsuited for gentle company. One *jäger* captain recorded:

As for the mountaineer, or the wild Scotch-Irish, this is a species of poor folk gathered from all nations of the world. They dwell in miserable log cabins, in the mountains three or four hundred miles from the seacoast, and live from the chase. Since these people usually maintain relations from the Indians, who are their neighbors, they take pains to assume a wild appearance, which results naturally from their rough manner of living. They are good and dangerous shooters, but a spirited bayonet charge gets them easily on their feet. They choose their own leaders and pay no attention to discipline. He who falls into their hands as prisoners seldom keeps anything more than what nature gave him at birth.

Lieutenant Colonel George Hanger offered an even less flattering opinion:

This distinguished race of men are more savage than the Indians, and possess every one of their vices, but **not one** of their virtues. I have known one of these fellows travel two hundred miles through

German illustration of an American rifleman (left) and Pennsylvania line (right), 1784.

the woods, never keeping any road or path, guided by the sun by day, and the stars by night, to kill a particular person belonging to the opposite party: he would shoot him before his own door, and ride away to boast of what he had done on his return. I speak only of the back-woodsmen, not of the inhabitants in general of South Carolina; for in all America, there are not better educated or better bred men than the planters. Indeed, Charlestown is celebrated for the splendour, luxury, and education of its inhabitants: I speak only of that heathen race known by the name of **Crackers**.

Impressed by their marksmanship, Continental Army Surgeon James Thacher wrote "These men are remarkable for the accuracy of their aim; striking a mark with great certainty at 200 yards distance. At a review, a company of them, while on quick advance, fired their balls into objects 7 inches diameter, at the distance of 250 yards." Portrait painter turned militia lieutenant Charles Wilson Peale noted in his diary, "One of [their] Captains who went to Relieve g[u]ard was shot at by three of our Riffle men at 250 yards distance & tumbled from his Horse, this is a practice which General Worshington now discoutenences."

Hanger's observation proved correct and the frontiersmen's insolence reached a peak when a rifle platoon marched on the guardhouse to free a comrade imprisoned there. Washington responded by ordering 500 men out with loaded guns and bayonets to secure the guardhouse. They were reinforced by another two regiments. Outnumbered and outgunned, the riflemen were disarmed, court martialed and fined. Despite this, when their term of enlistment neared expiration, Washington thought them "a useful corps" and asked Congress to find some means to induce them to extend their enlistment. When this failed, Washington turned to Daniel Morgan to raise a new rifle regiment drawn from existing regiments.

To counter the American riflemen, the British called upon their German allies to provide *jägers*. As woodsmen became accustomed to the rifle, great hope was placed on them. The British also called upon their loyalist allies, the Tories, to bring their rifles. Not well known is the fact the British distributed 1,000 pattern 1776 rifles among the different regiments. Perhaps the most innovative measure was by Major Patrick Ferguson, who designed a breechloading rifle based on the Chaumette rifle. Ferguson refined Chaumette's design by introducing a slight taper to the rotating breechplug that included cutouts for the fouling to collect into. Both innovations were supposed to handle the fouling that could jam an action. Ferguson demonstrated the effectiveness of his rifle before King George III by firing six shots in one minute and in so doing, missing his mark only once. With the king's approval, he had 100 of his rifles made and was permitted to draw men from various regiments to form his ad hoc rifle unit. Ferguson also arrived with green cloth from which his men's uniforms could be made.

Eventually the British abandoned Boston and on July 2, 1776, they landed 3,000 men on Staten Island in New York. They were reinforced on August 1 by a further 21,000, which included the Hessians and the *jägers*. On August 22, the British landed on Long Island. American Colonel Edward Hand's small rifle battalion (300) decided not to contest the larger British landing force but harassed the left flank as it moved inland. This precipitated the inevitable clash between themselves and the *jägers*, who earned the colonial rifleman's respect: "The idea which we were at first

Patrick Ferguson. Image courtesy of Kings Mountain National Military Park.

conceived of the Hessian riflemen was truly ridiculous, but the sad experiences convinces our people that they are an Enemy not to be despised." The *jägers* moved from tree to tree and fired from cover. One Hessian officer noted:

> The rebels have some very good marksmen, but some of them have wretched guns, and most of them shoot crooked. But they are clever at hunters' wiles. They climb trees, they crawl forward on their bellies for one hundred and fifty paces, shoot, and go as quickly back again. They make themselves shelters of bough, etc. But today they are much put out by our own green-coats, for we don't let our fellows fire unless they can get good aim at a man, so that they dare not undertake anything more against us.

Four days later, on August 26, William Howe launched his assault on Long Island. To pin the Americans, the Hessians and Highlanders maintained their post while Howe slipped around the Americans' left flank. Howe's attack routed the Americans and the Hessians caught many Americans at close quarters. One Hessian wrote: "The greater part of the riflemen were pierced with the bayonet to the trees. These dreadful people ought rather to be pitied than feared; they always require an quarter of an hour's time to load a rifle, and in the meantime they feel the effects of our balls and bayonets."

Howe did not follow up to capture the American Army on Long Island and the pause allowed the Americans to escape across the Hudson and regroup on Manhattan. On September 13, Howe landed on Manhattan and captured Harlem Heights. To flank

Like the Chaumette design that preceded it, **Ferguson's rifle** had a screw breech plug that was attached to the trigger guard. Ferguson's innovation included tapering the breech plug that reached the top of the barrel and introducing cleanout grooves cut into the threaded portion of the breech plug to collect the fouling and making the design less susceptible to jamming. To load the Ferguson, the user rotated the trigger guard 270°. This lowered the breech plug and exposed the barrel for loading. The ball was dropped into breech plug hole and was followed with powder. By rotating the trigger guard again, the breech plug rotated up, sealing the breach and pushing up any excess powder that was pushed (by hand) into the pan to prime it. Quicker loading than any contemporary rifle, the Ferguson was capable of taking a bayonet.

There were drawbacks and the Ferguson cost £4 as opposed to £2 for the Brown Bess. Another was the inherent weakness of the stock. Because a lot of wood was removed to accommodate the breech plug and the barrel extension for it, the stock was inherently weak and the two surviving examples in America both have cracks around the lock. The final issue with the Ferguson was its inadequate sealing of the breech and each discharge would be followed by gases escaping up from the breech plug. Producing the Ferguson needed industrial-age machinery in an era dominated by hand manufacturing. Gas sealing would not be solved until 1848 with the American Sharps breechloading rifle and later on, the metallic cartridge.

the Americans' position, Howe landed 4,000 men at Throg's Neck (Frog's Neck). Throg's Neck was not the ideal landing spot as there were only two usable paths from it to the mainland. American Colonel Edward Hand was posted at Throg's Neck with a mere 30 riflemen. Hand's men had earlier pulled up the planks on the bridge and fortified themselves on the opposite bank. The *jägers* and riflemen soon engaged in a lively exchange and Hand was reinforced with fresh units. Twenty-year-old Thomas Sullivan was there with the 49th Herefordshire and witnessed the fight between the riflemen and the *jägers*:

> They were within Gunshot of us on the other side of the gut; where they begin to Intrench themselves to our front; and kept continually firing at our advanced Sentries. ... The Chausseurs which are Excellent good Marksmen, and have all Riffle Barrels, were in the front and killed or wounded no less than 7 or 8 of ye Rebels a day across the Gut. They were sure if any man came within shot of them to hit him, if he was not under cover.

While the Hessians and other marksmen got the better of Hand's riflemen, Howe's plans were upset and after six days he re-embarked his troops and landed further north at White Plains. Eventually Washington was forced to abandon Manhattan Island.

British General John Burgoyne proposed a plan to divide the colonies by marching down the Hudson and isolating the rebellious New England colonies. He assembled a 9,500-strong invasion force that was to march south from Montreal toward Albany. It was to unite with a British army marching north along

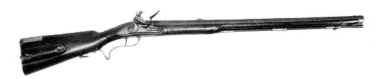

Jäger rifle. (West Point Collection)

the Hudson from New York: when the two met at Albany, the rebellious New England colonies would be isolated and could then be contained and crushed in detail.

The march started in the third week of June 1777 and proceeded very slowly as the British had to build their road through the wilderness. When the American army offered battle at Saratoga, Burgoyne's army had already been reduced to 6,000 men. Nonetheless he divided his army into three columns. The columns advanced over broken terrain, which made for poor communication and coordination between them.

The center column was a four-regiment-strong brigade under General Hamilton that bumped into Daniel Morgan's riflemen. Morgan's riflemen began picking off British officers in the advance guard. When the advance guard fell back, Morgan's men rushed forward only to be repulsed by Hamilton's main line. They fled like chickens before a fox and Morgan was almost in tears at the thought that his corps was destroyed. Sounding his rally cry, a turkey call, his men reassembled quickly around him and returned to battle. Reinforced by two line regiments, the battle became a fight over a clearing. As the British advanced, Morgan's men poured fire that broke the British who fled. Morgan's men would give chase, only to be met by the rallying British and their bayonets. The hunters were now the hunted and Morgan's men ran to the safety of their own infantry. So the battle went like a ship tossed about in the sea with one side chasing the other across the battlefield and in turn becoming the chased.

British Sergeant Roger Lamb recalled "[a] constant blaze of fire was kept up, and both armies seemed to be determined on death or victory ... Men and particularly officers, dropped every moment on each side. Several of the Americans placed themselves in high trees, and as often as they could distinguish a British officer's uniform, took him off by deliberately aiming at his person."

British artillery attempted to lay a suppressive fire against the Americans but they only brought themselves to the attention of Morgan's riflemen:

The Royal Artillery suffered an astonishing loss in today's action. One captain is dead; Captain Johns was fatally wounded and died on the next morning. Brigade Major Captain Bloomfield was shot through the cheek, under the tongue. General Phillips' other three adjutants were almost all wounded, as were some of General Burgoyne's. Somewhat more than thirty non-commissioned officers and artillerymen of the Royal Artillery were killed or wounded, of whom not a single man was less than five feet ten inches tall, all handsome individuals, of whom many died on the field of battle and were laid out in their true five feet eleven inches to six feet. Only one artillery officer was unwounded and 36 of the 48 artillery men were shot down.

Daniel Morgan.

Burgoyne was saved by his left wing, which was commanded by General Frederic von Riedesel. Riedesel, acting on his own initiative, marched his Hessians toward the sound of battle and provided Burgoyne the necessary manpower to drive the Americans from the field. The battle had cost the British 600 killed, wounded or captured. The Americans suffered 29 officers killed or wounded and 289 other casualties.

Eighteen days later, on October 7, Burgoyne was running low on supplies and was tired of waiting for the British force that was to march up from New York. Burgoyne was unaware that instead of marching north, Howe had embarked his men and sailed south to capture Philadelphia. Burgoyne decided to send a column to probe for the American left flank. He sent out two columns with General Riedesel leading one and General Simon Fraser the other.

At Bemis Heights, Fraser ran into Morgan's riflemen, who resumed picking off the British officers. As the British force began to fall into confusion and hesitate, Fraser rallied them. His gallantry was noted by American General Benedict Arnold who instructed Morgan to take his best men and kill him. Morgan described what followed in his backcountry manner of speech.

> Me and my boys had a bad time until I saw that they were led by an officer on a grey horse—a devilish brave fellow. Then says I to one of the best shots, says I, you get up into that there tree, and single out him on the horse. Dang it. Twas no sooner said than done. On came the British again, with the grey horseman leading; but his career was cut short enough this time. I jist tuck my eyes off him for a moment, and when I turned them to the place where he had been—pooh, he was gone!

With no one capable of rallying Fraser's men, they fell back to their redoubt with the Americans snapping at their heels. Rifleman Tim Murphy is generally given credit for shooting Fraser.

Following the battle Burgoyne eventually decided to retrace his steps to Canada. Progress was very slow and as the American forces swelled with reinforcements, Burgoyne offered a convention to American General Gates who accepted it. The significance of the victory is that French recognition followed and along with it, military aid and an alliance. It also meant that the American Revolution was now a world war, with the French fighting the British both in the East Indies and the Caribbean.

Believing that a British military presence would sway the southern colonies back into British fold, the British sent Culloden veteran Donald McDonald to North Carolina to rally the Highland immigrants. McDonald assembled over 1,600 men including 300 riflemen; many of whom had disdain for the Lowlanders who joined the rebels. Anticipating joining up with a British invasion force, McDonald marched his men toward the coast. As McDonald was sick, command was passed down to Colonel Donald McLeod, whose vanguard was eighty

Highlanders armed with broadswords. They were followed by another 1,000 men with the riflemen bringing up the rear. Many became disheartened along the march and deserted, reducing their number down to about 800.

Barring their path at Moore's Creek Bridge was Colonel James Moore with a smaller force of about 1,050 men. McLeod joined the vanguard and stormed the bridge. The American line exploded in gunfire and McLeod is said to have been pierced by twenty balls. The surviving Highlanders retreated and the American pursuit mopped up and arrested 850 loyalists. Many Highlanders refused to respond to subsequent Crown attempts to rally them. When the British force finally appeared off of Cape Fear, it found no loyalist force awaited them and so they sailed off to capture Charleston instead.

Guarding the entrance to Charleston Bay was the unfinished Fort Moultrie, on Sullivan's Island. Constructed of palmetto logs and sand, the men gallantly stood by their guns as nine British ships of the line attempted to bombard it into submission. To the surprise of the British, their cannon balls bounced off Moultrie's walls. Moultrie guns, on the other hand, mauled the ships.

Supporting the British seaborne attack was an overland operation that was to assault the fort from its unfinished rear. This was anticipated by the Americans whose cannons peppered the British as they landed. The survivors were greeted by rifle fire. One rifleman, Morgan Brown, described the fight: "Our rifles were in prime order, well proved and well charged; every man took deliberate aim at his object. . . . The fire taught the enemy to lie closer behind their bank of oyster shells, and only show themselves when they rose up to fire." One loyalist described being under fire: "It was impossible for any set of men to sustain so destructive a fire as the Americans poured in on this occasion."

Unable to capture Moultrie, the British departed and Charleston wasn't captured until 1780 when an 8,500-man force, including two companies of *jägers*, landed north of Charleston, marched inland and approached the peninsula from the north. They forced

American long rifle. (West Point Collection)

the Americans behind their fortifications and then besieged them. The *jägers* silenced the American artillery and according to one *jäger* officer, the Americans "tried to mask their embrasures with cowhides; however, as soon as a hide moved, the bullets of the *jägers* who were posted with cocked and leveled rifles, struck into the embrasure. I have lost only one workman from the 42nd, who was killed from a double-barreled blunderbuss from a house in the city, for we had chased the enemy away from behind their sandbags on the rampart." Upon surrender, he also wrote, "An enemy officer assured me that they suffered most from the *jägers* and the shell and small-arms fire, and that our rifles balls killed and wounded people in the rear works and even in the city." One *jäger* elaborated, "They confessed that since the opening of the third parallel our small-arms fire alone cost them between three and four hundred killed and wounded and that they could never open their embrasures without losses." With Charleston's fall the American southern army ceased to exist. Washington sent another army but it was crushed at Camden. A third under Nathaniel Green was sent to stop the British under Cornwallis on its march to recapture North Carolina. As he marched north, Cornwallis dispatched Patrick Ferguson with 1,000 musket-armed loyalists to protect his flank.

Ferguson had been injured at Brandywine in September 1777 when a musketball shattered his right elbow. With Ferguson absent, his ad hoc rifle unit had been disbanded and, as Howe put it, "this barbarous weapon"—Ferguson's breechloading rifle—was placed in storage. While he lost use of his right arm, Ferguson taught himself to write and fence with his left hand.

Refusing to be invalided home, Ferguson became a specialist in training provincial troops.

After being commanded to protect Cornwallis' flank, Ferguson boldly laid down the gauntlet, chastising the Americans for attacking the King's outposts and warned them to desist lest he "hang their leaders and lay waste their country with fire and sword." Instead of cowering, the backwoodsmen became outraged and assembled a force larger than Ferguson's to march against him. Learning that he was outnumbered, Ferguson retreated to a hilltop called Kings Mountain where he felt himself perfectly capable of defending himself until reinforced. Instead, on October 7, 1780, the American riflemen crushed Ferguson's loyalists and killed Ferguson. It was a triumph of a mostly rifle-armed force against a musket-armed one.

The American army shattered at Camden was still recovering when its commander, Green, divided it in the face of the enemy. He kept the larger wing and organized the other into a flying column led by Daniel Morgan. Morgan's column was 120 miles away from Green's army when he learned that the feared British Legion had been dispatched to crush him. In a battle that should have been another British victory, Morgan used every disadvantage to his advantage and instead crushed his enemy at Cowpens on January 17, 1781. Morgan posted his riflemen in the front line and instructed them to shoot the officers. Afterward they were to retreat uphill past Morgan's second line, which was composed of militia. Knowing the militia's propensity to run, Morgan had instructed them to fire two volleys before retreating behind his third line, which was composed of discharged Continental regulars.

The British advanced to within 50 yards before the riflemen dutifully picked off the officers and sergeants before retreating. As the British continued advancing, the men of the militia discharged two volleys before they too retreated. Thinking the Americans were fleeing, order was lost as the British broke into pursuit. Somewhat disorganized, they were stopped by a volley from the Continentals who stood their ground. The British re-formed and began returning volleys. When the British began a flanking movement, the Americans responded by refusing the flank. Other Americans mistook this as a retreat and started pulling back. Encouraged by what looked the American line collapsing, the British surged forward again and came within 50 yards of the Americans who suddenly spun around and fired a volley. They then lowered their bayonets and charged the stunned British, attacking them from both the front and their flank. British resistance collapsed in a stunning loss.

Despite the two setbacks at Kings Mountain and Cowpens, Cornwallis continued into North Carolina until he caught up with and defeated Green at Guilford Court House. It was a pyrrhic victory since Cornwallis suffered huge casualties himself. After resting on the battlefield, Cornwallis decided to march into Virginia where he could be reinforced and replenished by the Royal Navy.

As Cornwallis marched north from South Carolina, American forces under Lieutenant Colonel "Lighthorse" Harry Lee and Lieutenant Colonel Francis "Swamp Fox" Marion began attacking various British outposts. After an unsuccessful siege of Fort Ninety-Six, the Americans withdrew because of the approaching relief column. Despite a successful defense, Ninety-Six was abandoned, allowing the Americans to drive forward. They next attacked Fort Watson that was built atop an Indian mound on the Santee River. Lacking cannons and entrenching tools, they were unable to besiege it and instead used an innovation suggested by South Carolina's Major Hezekiah Maham. They felled trees for logs and built a log tower that was filled with dirt and stones and a firing platform on top. Upon the tower's completion, riflemen were posted to fire down into the fort. Since the defending British and loyalists lacked artillery with which they could knock the tower down, they found themselves defenseless and surrendered. This tactic was repeated successfully at Forts Granby, Galpin, and Augusta. The fall of these forts disrupted British communications with the interior and after September 1781 the British held only the coastal region of South Carolina.

Fort Sackville, near modern-day Vincennes, Indiana, was a base from which the British supplied their Indians who raided Virginia's frontier region. Virginian George Rogers Clark petitioned Governor Patrick Henry for permission to raise a 500-strong force to raid the British outposts at Kaskaskia and Fort Sackville. After securing his commission, Clark raised only 175 men for his expedition. He captured Kaskaskia before marching on Fort Sackville. Lacking cannons, Clark's men used the cover of darkness to dig pits close to the fort. At dawn, his men began firing into the fort's loopholes and cannon ports. The pits were too close to the fort for the cannons to be depressed sufficiently and cannonballs sailed harmlessly over Clark's men, while anyone who exposed himself at a cannon port was instantly fired upon by Clark's riflemen. The fort's defenders replied ineffectively with musketry. To prompt the British to surrender, Clark had four Indians tomahawked in view of the fort. Clark then warned that he could not promise to restrain his men when they stormed the fort. Intimidated, the British surrendered and only afterward learned that Clark's force, which they had believed larger than their own, was about equal in size.

French intervention finally tipped the scale against the British. At Chesapeake Bay, the French naval squadron drove off the Royal Navy, leaving Cornwallis isolated. Trapped at Yorktown, Cornwallis wanted a battle but Washington, acting on the advice of Rochambeau, laid siege instead and Cornwallis was starved into submission. While no more battles were fought in America, the war had become a global conflict with Spain and the Netherlands also fighting the British. It was another two years before the Treaty of Paris restored peace.

CHAPTER 2

RIFLES WIN ACCEPTANCE

1797–1815

"Where the musket ends, the rifle begins."

By 1789, with the exception of Great Britain and the United States which had disbanded all rifle units in 1783, almost all armies had adopted the rifle in limited numbers. The British corrected this situation in 1797 when several understrength Germanic units were merged to become the rifle-armed 5/60 Royal Americans. They were followed shortly thereafter by Coote Manningham's Experimental Corps of Riflemen, which was drawn from various regiments. Trained as skirmishers and as riflemen, they fought at Ferrol in 1800 before being disbanded. The decision was reached to have a permanent rifle regiment and most officers of the Experimental Corps of Rifles were retained. New men were brought in and the unit became the Rifle Corps, later numbered the 95th Regiment and styled as the Rifle Brigade.

Besides being trained to fight as line infantry, they were also trained as expert skirmishers, in picketing, scouting, and patrolling. They became adept marksmen and some men held the targets for the others at 150–200 yards. This was inherently dangerous and there was one accident when the target holder was shot by an officer who had taken a man's rifle so as to instruct the men. Like the Brunswick Oels or elements of the King's German Legion, the 95th were intended to serve in the vanguard and drive off their French counterparts, the voltigeurs and tirailleurs. The 95th earned its laurels in Monte Video, Uruguay, in 1807.

We turn to one rifleman in particular who exemplified the best and the worst qualities of a soldier, Tom Plunkett. Plunkett was born in Newton County, Ireland, and at age twenty he enlisted in the Rifle Brigade on May 10, 1805. Described as a "smart, well-made fellow, about middle height and in the prime of manhood; with clear grey eyes and handsome countenance," he was believed by some to be the "best shot in the regiment." In his book Random Shots From a Rifleman, Kincaid described Plunkett as: "… a bold, active, athletic Irishman, and a deadly shot …" Initially sent to South America in 1807 under Lieutenant General John Whitelocke, Plunkett began to build his reputation as a rifleman there.

Whitelocke's reinforcements of four companies of the 1/95 were united with the three companies of the 2/95 and placed under the command of Major McLeod as a provisional battalion. Along with the army, they pushed onto Buenos Aires and stormed the town. However, poor leadership failed to consolidate the victory and the Spaniards rallied, and isolating the scattered British units, successively forced them to surrender. In one of the isolated British units was Tom Plunkett, who was kept very active:

> In an action to retake Buenos Aires, he and Fisher, another rifleman, were hoisted onto the roof of a low building to act as sharpshooters. Some years later, when asked by an officer of the 95th how many men he had killed from this position, Plunkett replied: "Twenty, sir," then added: "I shot a gentleman with a flag of truce, sir." Not understanding the situation, that is exactly what he had done, and the man had died of his wounds.

Along with the rest of the army, Plunkett was captured and paroled to England. Rejoining the 1st Battalion, he was sent to the Spanish peninsula under Sir John Moore where Plunkett distinguished himself, as described by Kincaid:

Rifleman of the 95th Regiment, Napoleonic era.

The regiment was formed in front of Calcabellos covering the rear of the infantry, and on the first appearance of the enemy they had been ordered to withdraw behind the town. Three parts of them had already passed the bridge, and the remainder were upon it, or in the act of filing through the street with the careless confidence which might be expected from their knowledge that the British cavalry still stood between them and the enemy; but in an instant our own cavalry, without the slightest notice, galloped through and over them, and the same instant saw a French sabre flourishing over the head of every man who remained beyond the bridge—many were cut down in the streets, and a great portion of the rear company were taken prisoners.

The remainder of the regiment, seeing the unexpected attack, quickly drew off among the vineyards to the right and left of the road, where they coolly awaited the approaching assaults. The dismounted voltigeurs first swarmed over the river, assailing the riflemen on all sides, but they were met by a galling fire which effectively stopped them. General Colbert next advanced to dislodge them, and passing the river at the head of his dragoons, he charged furiously up the road; but, when within a few yards of our own men, he was received with such a deadly fire, that scarcely a Frenchman remained in the saddle, and the general himself was among the slain. The voltigeurs persevered in their unsuccessful endeavors to force the post, and a furious fight continued to be waged, until darkness put an end to it, both sides having suffered severely ...

General Colbert (the enemy's hero of the day), was, by all accounts, (if I may be permitted the expression,) splendid as a man; and not less so as a soldier. From the commencement of the retreat of our army he had led the advance, and been conspicuous for his daring: his gallant bearing had, in fact, excited the admiration of his enemies; but on this day, the last of his brilliant earthly career, he was mounted on a white charger, and had been a prominent figure in the attack of our men in the street the instant before, and it is not, therefore, to be wondered at if the admiration for the soldier was for a space drowned in the feeling for the fallen comrades which his bravery had consigned to death; a rifleman, therefore, of the name of Plunkett, exclaiming, "thou too shalt surely die!" took up an advanced position, for the purpose of singling him out, and by his hand he no doubt fell.

1/95 Rifleman Costello places the location at Astorga and elaborated:

[A] French General named Colbert, conspicuous on a grey horse, was remarkably active. Although frequently aimed at by our men, he seemed to bear a charmed life, and invariably escaped. In one of the French charges headed by this daring officer, General Sir Edward Paget rode up to the rifles and offered his purse to any man who would shoot him. Plunkett immediately started from his company. He ran about a hundred yards nearer to the enemy, threw himself on his back on the road (which was covered with snow), placed his foot in the sling of his rifle, and taking deliberate aim, shot General Colbert. Colbert's Trumpet-Major, who rode up to him, shared the same fate from Tom's unerring rifle. Our men, who had been anxiously watching, cheered, and Tom began running in upon the rearmost sections. He was just in time to escape some dozen troopers who had chased after him.

Our General immediately gave Tom the purse he had promised with encomiums upon his gallantry. He promised to recommend him to his Colonel, which he did in high terms to Colonel Beckwith. A few days afterwards, when the French attacked Sir John Moore's position at Corunna, Plunkett was again noted for his cool bravery and daring, especially in making admirable shots, by which they lost many officers.

While Rifle Brigade historian Sir William Cope doubted whether Paget would order a rifleman to deliberately shoot down an enemy officer, Marshal Soult complained that it was British policy to shoot officers. If Paget had indeed bartered for Colbert's death, he certainly was not alone. Incentive to shoot officers also arose from the desire to gain plunder which came from purse, jewelry and the lace that adorned their uniforms—lace was useful for barter.

The retreat to Corunna saw the Rifle Brigade and Tom Plunkett return to England in early 1809. The campaign had been difficult and many suffered from starvation during the retreat. Weapons were rusted and needed repairs or replacement. Their lice-infested clothes were thrown in a pile and burned. Plunkett was recognized by being promoted to corporal by Colonel Beckwith. Having been depleted, the regiment needed to recruit and Plunkett was among those chosen for this task. One stunt he demonstrated was the ease with which his green uniform could be kept, unlike the redcoat worn by most British infantry with its white crossbelts that were difficult to keep spotless. Plunkett would descend a chimney, brush himself off and present himself ready for inspection by his recruits. The regiment's recruitment efforts not only filled the existing two battalions but also raised enough for a third. All three accompanied Wellington back to the peninsula.

Plunkett rose to sergeant but, falling victim to drink, defied the order of a more senior sergeant. Captain James H. K. Stewart (1st Company, 1/95), confined Plunkett to his quarters under arrest. Angered, Plunkett loaded about a dozen rifles and placing

The Baker rifle was used by British rifle regiments during the Napoleonic Wars.

himself at a window, waited for Captain Stewart. Another officer intervened and convinced Plunkett to surrender. Sobered, Plunkett expressed his regrets. However, the gravity of his crime could not go unpunished and sentencing included demotion and three hundred lashes (he received only thirty-five before Colonel Beckwith stopped administration). Plunkett recovered soon enough and regained his status as a favorite of the officers and became a corporal again. Plunkett survived the Peninsular campaign and fought at Waterloo where he was injured on the forehead. Discharged on November 10, 1817 for "bad character," he purportedly enlisted in a redcoat regiment and came across his old colonel, now General, Sir Sidney Beckwith. Plunkett emigrated to Canada where the government settled some pensioners, but finding it not to his liking, returned to England where he died in 1850.

The King's German Legion

During the Napoleonic Wars (1803–15), Hanover was still a British possession and when England was at war with Napoleon, it naturally drew on its German subjects. Some of these units were partially armed with rifles, such as the King's German Legion or the Brunswicks Oels. Serving in the 2nd Battalion of the King's German Legion was Friedrich Lindau. A weaver's son, he was apprenticed to a shoemaker and at age twenty-one ran away from his home in Hamelin, Hanover, to England where he enlisted as a rifleman. Lindau was quite a rogue but this did not impair his fighting qualities. In 1811, he left with his battalion to fight under Wellington in the Peninsular campaign. Having looted and fought his way during the Spanish peninsula, he was part of Wellington's army that invaded France in 1813–14. During the siege of Bayonne, he had the opportunity to shoot a French officer:

Recruitment poster for the 95th Regiment.

One morning I stood at this outpost and conversed with the French opposite and went into the garden to pick some flowers, which the French did not stop me from doing. About three of them, who had crept up, immediately fired, the bullets whistled over me, but with one bound I was out of the garden and standing in front of the house, just as an English officer stepped out and gave me a strong rebuke.

At midday on the same day (my anger at the reprimand I got and the cunning of the French was still fresh in my mind) I said to Captain Lindam [his company commander], who was at the outpost: "It is not fair that we are not allowed to shoot at all and the French constantly fire on us if we put in an appearance."

"It must not happen," he said, "it is strictly forbidden."

"I will not refrain from shooting if I surprise one," was my answer. The captain turned round and went away without answering me. So I believed I had a half "Yes", took my rifle and crawled into the trench nearest the fortress; one detached house in front of it was occupied by the French. A French officer had shot at us from it from time to time for some days with a long rifle; I aimed at him. I had removed the round from my rifle, taken double powder, put a ball with a patch on, and I lay down at the lookout after I had crawled a certain distance nearer behind a little mound.

I had lain there a good hour when the officer came to the window. He put his rifle in place and took aim; I pulled my trigger and in a moment saw, with indescribable joy, my man fall out of the window. I hurried back, but remained lying in the trench because I saw that our company had to form up. Immediately Adjutant Riefkugel and the brigade major came and held an inquiry, but they went away again when our captain told them nothing had happened. When they had gone away I crawled out of the trench and got a reprimand from the captain. But when I looked at him and saw how glad he was that he had seen the officer fall from the window, I replied, "That fellow will never shoot again." After the surrender of Bayonne some Germans from the garrison came into our camp and asked who had fired at this officer; I was called in and then they told me that they had just sat down at the table in the barrack room, my bullet had pierced the dish and all their soup spilt upon the table.

Lindau fought at Waterloo and was among the defenders of La Haye Sainte: "New regiments were continually brought up but regularly beaten back. An enemy officer fell to me nearby; he had been constantly riding round the battlefield in front of us and showing the way to the advancing columns. For some time I had him in my sights—at last, just as he was leading up new troops, he came into my fire. His horse made a bound, reared up and fell with the rider beneath it." During a counterattack, Lindau looted the officer. Subsequently, Lindau was shot in the head but had a comrade pour rum on a handkerchief and tie it around his head. An officer ordered him to retire but he replied, "No, so long as I can stand I stay at my post." He continued fighting until he was captured (and relieved of his loot). For his bravery exhibited in the Peninsular campaign and at Waterloo, Lindau received the Guelphic Medal. He was discharged for his injuries on October 24, 1816.

The War of 1812

After the two (1812) failed American attempts to invade Canada, American General William Harrison began building Fort Meigs on the east bank of the Maumee River in Ohio. It was incomplete when it was besieged by British General Henry Proctor and a large force of Indians under Tecumseh. Proctor's men erected a battery and commenced shelling the fort. Meanwhile Tecumseh's Indians surrounded the other three sides of the fort to contain the defenders.

From the west bank of the Maumee, one Indian sharpshooter climbed an elm tree and began annoying the defenders. As the fort was unfinished and the wells weren't dug, the men had to go 100 yards to the river for water. Since the Indian was shooting at 600 yards distance, the defenders joked about it. The common belief was that he was too far to be a serious threat and it was not worth the powder to reply. After a few days' practice, the Indian figured out the hold and injured two men. All joking stopped and Elijah Kirk of William Sebree's Co. of Boswell's Regiment, Kentucky Detached Militia, requested permission to retaliate. His officer insisted it was too far and a waste of powder. After a third soldier was injured, Kirk was granted permission.

Finding a rest in a blockhouse, Kirk observed the tree and waited for his opportunity. A discharge of smoke from the tree announced that the Indian had fired again. Observing the smoke, Kirk determined the wind's drift and fired. Eyes riveted to the tree in suspense. Then, a rifle dropped, soon followed by the Indian himself. The besieging force had lost its finest marksman. Both the unnamed Indian and Kirk were remarkable marksmen and their shots exceeded all prior records. Fort Meigs held and the British invasion was thwarted.

Revolutionary War British Colonel George Hanger discusses hitting targets at that distance: "Reader, do not be surprised at my speaking of 600 yards practice,—for I do not mean to say, that I can hit a horse or an elephant at that distance; but I will prove to you, that I can throw a ball into a piece of canvas six feet high by fifteen feet long; and this will prove that a ball may be thrown, at that distance, into a column of troops on their line of march." Skeptics may balk but in the 1930s Walter Cline proved it possible. Cline used a rifle rebored to about .53 caliber. The first shot at 600 yards went one foot below the target and out of ten shots, four struck with the six misses being close.

After Napoleon abdicated in 1814, veteran British troops were freed for offensive operations in America. British strategy was no different from that of the American Revolution. Basically, it called for dividing the states. One army was to follow Burgoyne's plan of isolating the New England states by seizing Lake Champlain and the Hudson Valley region. The advance along Lake Champlain ended when the American flotilla defeated the British naval squadron. Without command of the lake, the British withdrew. A second army, serving as a diversion from Canada, was to sail up the Chesapeake and attack Washington, D.C. They quickly scattered the militia forces at the battle of Bladensburg and burned Washington. After the unsuccessful siege of Fort McHenry, the offensive faltered when, during a march to capture Baltimore, Major General Robert Ross was shot on September 12, 1814, by sharpshooters. At dispute is whether Ross was shot by sharpshooters Daniel Wells and Henry McComas, both of whom were killed in the skirmish before the battle of North Point (September 12, 1814), or by the Fifth Regiment's Independent Blues or the Mechanical Volunteers. Most British sources credit Ross' death to riflemen and one British newspaper called Ross' death: "the assassin-like manoeuver of marking their man, under the security of their impenetrable forests." What is significant is that Ross' death left the British land forces without energetic leadership to capture Baltimore, thus sparing that city. The third army, led by Peninsular War veteran Sir Edward Pakenham, was to capture New Orleans and isolate the interior.

Sir Edward Pakenham arrived from Jamaica with his army on December 13, 1815. While surveying the American positions at New Orleans, Pakenham nearly had an encounter with the

American rifleman and, but for the quick eye of one of his aides, could have succumbed before the battle. Sir Harry Smith was assigned to Sir Edward as assistant adjutant general and observed: "The Staff were very near the enemy's line, when I saw some riflemen evidently creeping down and not farther off than a hundred yards, and so I very abruptly said, 'Ride away, Sir Edward, behind this bank or you will be shot in a second. By your action you will be recognized as the Commander in Chief, and some riflemen are now going to fire.'" Sir Harry saved his commander but not for long. Attesting to the skill of the American frontier rifleman, we have this account by an anonymous British officer who fought there:

"We marched," said this officer, "in solid column in a direct line, upon the American defenses. I belonging to the staff; and as we advanced, we watched through our glasses, the position of the enemy, with that intensity an officer only feels when marching into the jaws of death. It was a strange sight, that breastwork, with the crowds of beings behind, their heads only visible above the line of defense. We could distinctly see the long rifles lying on the works, and the batteries in our front with their great mouths gaping towards us. We could see the position of General Jackson, with his staff around him. But what attracted our attention most was the figure of a tall man standing on the breastworks dressed in linsey-woolsey, with buckskin leggins and a broad-brimmed hat that fell around his face almost concealing his features. He was standing in one of those picturesque graceful attitudes peculiar to those natural men dwelling in forests. The body rested on the left leg and swayed with a curved line upward. The right arm was extended, the hand grasping the rifle near the muzzle, the butt of which rested near the toe of his right foot. With his left hand he raised the rim of his hat from his eyes and seemed gazing intently on our advancing column. The cannon of the enemy had opened up on us and tore through our ranks with dreadful slaughter; but we continued to advance unwavering and cool, as if nothing threatened our program.

"The roar of the cannon had no effect upon the figure before us; he seemed fixed and motionless as a statute. At last he moved, threw back his hat rim over the crown with his left hand, raised his rifle and took aim at our group. At whom had he leveled his piece? But the distance was so great that we looked at each other and smiled. We saw the rifle flash and very rightly conjectured that his aim was in the direction of our party. My right hand companion, as noble a fellow as ever rode at the head of a regiment, fell from his saddle. The hunter paused a few moments without moving the gun from his shoulder. Then he reloaded and resumed his former attitude. Throwing the hat rim over his eyes and again holding it up with the left hand, he fixed his piercing gaze upon us, as if hunting out another victim. Once more, the hat rim was thrown back, and the gun raised to his shoulder. This time we did not smile, but cast our glances at each other, to see which of us must die. When again the rifle flashed another of our party dropped to the earth. There was something most awful in this marching to certain death. The cannon and thousands of musket balls played upon our ranks, we cared not for; for there was a chance of escaping them. Most of us had walked as coolly upon batteries more destructive without quailing, but to know that every time that rifle was leveled toward us that one of us must surely fall; to see it rest motionless as if poised on a rack, and know when the hammer came down that the messenger of death drove unerringly to its goal, to know this and still march on, was awful.

"I could see nothing but the tall figure standing on the breastworks; he seemed to grow, phantom-like, higher and higher, assuming through the smoke the supernatural appearance of some great spirit of death. Again did he reload and discharge and reload and discharge his rifle with the same unfailing aim, and the same unfailing result; and it was with indescribable pleasure that I beheld, as we marched [toward] the American lines, the sulphorous clouds gathering around us, and shutting that spectral hunter from our gaze.

"We lost the battle, and to my mind, that Kentucky Rifleman contributed more to our defeat than anything else; for while he remained to our sight, our attention was drawn from our duties. And when at last, we became enshrouded in the smoke, the work was completed, we were in utter confusion and unable, in the extremity, to restore order sufficient to make any successful attack."

James Tandy Ellis of the Filson Club of Louisville, Kentucky later "made long inquiry and search for the name of this Kentucky rifleman, and at last found that his name was E. M. Brank of Greenville, Kentucky, and … found his grave at Greenville." Ephraim McLean Brank was born in Greenville, on August 1, 1790 to Robert Brank and Margaret McLean. He studied law and during the war served as a lieutenant in the Kentucky Detached Militia. After the war, Brank returned to Greenville and resumed his practice before passing away in 1875 at age eighty-four.

Several questions come to mind. Is there corroborating evidence? Why wasn't Brank himself shot? At what distance did Brank commence firing, and, finally, is there any truth to this fabulous tale? Turning to our first question, a variation has been found from another source:

> An interesting note came from a newspaper in 1840 (entitled Anecdote of the Battle of New Orleans): "A daring Tennessean, with a blanket tied around him, and a hat with a brim of enormous breadth, who seemed to be fighting on his own hook, disdaining to raise his rifle over the bank of earth and fire, in safety to his person, like his more wary fellow soldiers, chose to spring, every time he fired upon the breast work, where balancing himself he would bring his rifle to cheek, throw back his broad brim, take sight and fire, while the enemy were advancing to attack, as deliberate as though shooting at a herd of deer; then leaping down the other side he would reload mount the works, cock his beaver, take aim and crack again."
>
> "This he did"; said an English officer who was taken prisoner, and who laughingly related it as a good anecdote; "five times in rapid succession as I advanced at the head of my company. Though the grape whistled over our heads, for the life of me, I could not help smiling at the grotesque demi-savage, demi-quaker figure, as he threw back the broad flap of his castor to obtain a fair sight— deliberately raise his rifle, shut his left eye, and blaze away at us. I verily believe he brought down one of my men at every shot."

Whether this account is merely an elaboration by an imaginative writer or more details from the same observer is difficult to gauge. Notable differences include the reference to jumping up and down from the breastworks and the closing of the left eye. The latter would be difficult to see at a distance or through the haze of battle.

On the next issue, how could the British 3/95 riflemen who outfought Napoleon's finest skirmishers overlook a solitary figure standing atop the breastworks? It is unthinkable that they would ignore a prime target. For an explanation, we turn to Sir Harry Smith of Pakenham's staff: "The American riflemen are very slow, though most excellent shots." While marksmanship is vital, 3/95 Quartermaster Williams Surtees provides details: "[T]he enemy had been quite prepared, and opened such a heavy fire upon the different columns, and upon our skirmishers, (what had been formed for some time within 100 or 150 yards of the enemy's works,) as it is not easy to conceive." If we accept Pickles' figure of 2,032 American riflemen to 546 British, or four to one, Surtees' comment is not unreasonable.

Furthermore, Surtees provides another insight that increases this disparity: "The right column, under General Gibbs, was to consist of the 4th, 21st, 44th, and three companies of my battalion. ... The left column, commanded by General Keene, was to be composed as follows, viz.—one company of the 7th, one of the 21st, one of the 43d, and two of ours." This division further reduced the number of British riflemen facing American

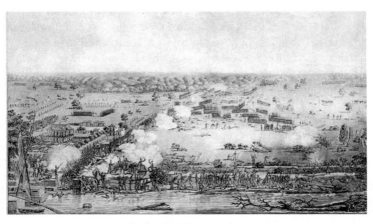

The battle of New Orleans.

riflemen and increased the ratio enjoyed by the Americans to 9:1 (2,232 v. 239). Corroborating Surtees is Sir Harry: "Never since Bueno Ayres had I witnessed a reverse, and the sight to our eyes, which had looked on victory so often, was appalling indeed. ... The fire, I admit, was the most murderous I ever held before or since ..." This was quite a compliment considering Sir Harry had fought the Spaniards in Argentina, the Dutch, the French in Spain and Waterloo, and had seen action in South Africa (Sixth Cape Frontier War) and in India where he was knighted. Simply put, there were more American riflemen present and they simply overwhelmed their British counterparts who not only had to contend with them, but also with the American artillery. One British officer wrote: "The rifle-corps individually took post to resist any forward movement of the enemy, but the ground already named being under a cross fire of at least twenty pieces of artillery, the advantage was all on the side of the Americans."

The other question concerned the distance from which Brank commenced firing and again Sir Harry provides a clue. Detailed to a party tasked with burying their dead, Sir Harry noted: "A more appalling spectacle cannot be conceived than this common grave. The Colonel, Butler, was very sulky if I tried to get near the works. This scene was not more that about eighty yards away from them ..." A British column marching at ordinary pace covers 62½ yards per minute (30-inch pace at 75 paces per minute). It would take over six minutes for a column to advance over 400 yards. The column however, stopped to return fire. Sir Harry reported: "[H]ad our heaviest column rushed forward in place of halting to fire under a fire fifty times superior, our national honour would not have been tarnished, but have gained fresh lustre." Lieutenant John Henry Cooke, 43rd Infantry, fought at New Orleans and confirms the British halted and fired. "As this column neared the American lines, the musketry opened on them while crossing the drains which here and there intersected these flats; and as there was not the least cover, the troops began to suffer much, and opened a heavy fire of musketry, which positively obliged the rifles which led them to cling to the earth." "Rifles" as used by Cooke is in reference to the 3/95 riflemen, who were suppressed by their own supporting infantry! It was at 80 yards distance from the American position that most British soldiers fell and were buried. Furthermore, 80 yards is generally beyond the effective range of musket-armed soldiers.

With the exception of Brank, the Americans weren't offering a "figure of a man" and only their heads were visible from behind the earthworks. As at Breed's Hill during the American Revolution, the British column stopped to fire when it should have rushed forward. While it is possible that Brank commenced firing from 400 yards distance, this isn't plausible considering Brank was shooting offhand. For steadiness, rifle shooting with a roundball flintlock rifle at 300–400 yards is generally done either prone or lying upon one's back. During the American Revolution a bugler, whose horse was both behind and between that of Lieutenant Colonels Banastre Tarleton and George Hanger, was shot from 400 yards by a rifleman who "laid himself down on his belly; for, in such positions, they always lie, to make a good shot at a long distance." Given that Brank fired at least four times and that it takes about a minute to reload, or three minutes altogether for three reloads, the column would have, at ordinary pace, advanced 187½ yards. Add the 80 yards for where most soldiers fell and we attain a minimal distance of 267.5 yards. Since Brank "resumed his former attitude" after his first shot, some distance must be added and how much more is left to conjecture.

British Captain J. Nelson Cooke described the devastating effect of American rifle fire:

Subsequent examination of the field gave a clue to the cause of the panic. It was the wonderful accuracy and murderous effect of the American fire. The casualties by cannon was very few. Nearly all fell to rifles. Of those killed an appalling proportion particularly at the point nearest the lines were shot through the head. The American hunting rifles carried small balls. One of our ounce musket balls melted up and poured in their molds would make three of them. But through the head or viscera they were as fatal as any. Hitting the face or forehead, life went out as the ball went in! I had seen many battlefields in Spain and the East, fresh with carnage. But no where had been such a scene as the spot where the Forty-fourth was butcher'd.

We turn now to the final question of whether a solitary rifleman could wreak such havoc. Surtees who, "was not in it ... but I was so posted as to see it plainly," provides corroboration: "[T]he right column never reached the

5/60 Rifleman (left) and 95 Rifleman (right) during Napoleonic Wars

point to which it was directed; but from the dreadful fire of every kind poured into it, some of the battalions began to waver, to halt and fire, and at last one of them completely broke, and became disorganized." One British officer wrote: "On our right again, the Twenty-First and Forty-fourth being almost cut to pieces, and thrown into some confusion by the enemy's fire, the Ninety-third pushed up and took the lead." Before the battle Sir Harry noted: "The soldiers were sulky, and neither the 21st nor the 44th were distinguished for discipline—certainly not of the sort I had been accustomed to." Seeing the 44th waver, Pakenham cried out, "Lost for the want of courage," rode off to rally them, and was mortally wounded.

Numerous newspaper accounts provide the same account and it was repeated as late as July 10, 1861, in Virginia's *Richmond Dispatch*. Another source is the (non-contemporary) diary of Isaac Bard who researched the history of Muhlenberg County, where Brank originated, and wrote: "It is said that Ephraim Brank and Edward Jarvis mounted the breastworks and there fired into the British army, as they marched up, as fast as their friends could load the rifles for them. I can see it stated lately in a highly respectable paper that Mr. Brank brought down several British officers in their march up to our breastworks at the battle below New Orleans …"

Clearly Brank did not repel the entire column single-handedly and he had the support of cannons as well as over two thousand other riflemen. This does not belittle Brank's achievement but places it into perspective. His was the "influence on the mind" that broke resolve. With its officers terror-stricken, the men leaderless and demoralized, it is easy to see why the British column broke. British casualties being over 33 percent (2,100 killed or wounded and over five hundred captured), the prowess earned by the Revolutionary War American rifleman was not tarnished by their heirs at New Orleans. The British Medical Director's casualty report included an interesting observation: "Of the total number (3,325) about three thousand were struck by small bullets of the type American sharpshooters used in their rifles; the rest (about 325) by missiles of artillery or by the ounce balls used in regulation muskets."

CHAPTER 3

PERCUSSION ERA AND THE MINIÉ BALL
1817–57

"The Frenchmen were shot down helplessly by an unseen enemy."

Technological advances

FRUSTRATED THAT THE FLINTLOCK'S FLASH STARTLED game birds, Scottish clergyman Alexander Forsyth discovered the explosive property of fulminate of mercury as a means of ignition and patented his invention in 1807. Several clumsy attempts were made to adapt Forsyth's discovery to firearms and only after Joshua Shaw placed a small dab of it into a copper cup, called a percussion cap, was its potential realized. The cap was placed onto a nipple that was screwed into the bolster. The nipple was bored out such that when the hammer struck the cap, the cap sent a flame down the nipple and through the bolster and from the bolster to the barrel's powder charge. Since they were more reliable and less prone to failure in the rain than flintlocks, percussion-fired firearms were adopted universally.

Bullet design was not stagnant either. In 1838 the French in Algiers found themselves coming under long-range fire from the

Hythe School of Musketry, 1855.

Arab natives, whose firearms had aperture sights with several holes, each at a different height from its base and this gave the user the ability to accommodate for a varying distances. In 1838 the Duke of Orléans was annoyed by the long-range fire of an Arab sheik. He offered 5 francs to any man who could bring the Arab down. One chasseur stepped out of the ranks and after taking careful aim fired and killed him at 650 yards. What made this feat possible was a new gun invented by Captain Gustave H. Delvigne which had a powder chamber smaller than the bore. An undersized ball was dropped down the barrel and then smashed to fit the grooves by pounding it with a ramrod. Since each soldier rammed the ball down differently, inconsistent results were yielded.

Delvigne's design was superseded by one by Colonel Thouvenin whose breech had a stud, or tige (anvil) as he called it, protruding from the bottom of the breechplug. The bullet itself was undersized to the bore and cylindrical-conical shape with a flat bottom. After inserting the conical bullet down the barrel, the soldier struck it three times with the ramrod to expand it to fit the rifling. Englishman W. W. Greener designed an undersized two-piece that when fired, drove the plug into the ball, causing it to expand and fit the rifling.

Surpassing them all was the minié ball. Named after French Captain Claude Minié, it was an undersized conical bullet with a hollow base that contained an iron cup. When the gun was fired, the cup forced the bullet to expand to fill the bore. Like Greener's design, it was undersized and didn't need any number of taps to seat and expand it. A rifle firing the minié ball could be loaded as quickly as the musket and was more accurate than the round-ball rifle. However if the iron base was lost, the minié would not expand. Across the pond in America, Harper's Ferry armorer James Burton found that by thinning the base of the minié ball, the same expansion could be had without needing an iron cup or plug. It was now possible to arm every soldier with a rifle with the potential to hit a man-sized target at 450 meters. To take advantage of the minié rifle's potential, instructional shooting schools like Vincennes in France or Hythe in England sprung up to train soldiers on how to use it. Their instructional books did reach America, but only enjoyed a limited readership. The final innovations of the era were in optics and sights. Prismatic teleometers (monoscopes) with stadia lines for rangefinding were developed and around 1861 bubble spirit level sights were introduced. The latter allowed the user to determine at a glance whether his firearm was canted.

The Crimean War

War with Russia provided a convenient testing ground for the new guns. When the British advanced on Sevastopol, the 2/95 screened their advance. On October 23, 1853, Rifleman Henry Herbert spotted a Russian officer riding a white horse. After adjusting his sights, he shot the officer who fell from his horse. Herbert thought the distance was 1,000 yards but upon pacing the distance, discovered it was 1,300. More Russian losses from long-range fire followed and Russian General Menshilkov noted, "The sharpshooting of the English riflemen caused our troops terrible losses." Joining him in his complaint was General Edward Todleben: "At the Alma their infantry, armed with smooth-bores, could not hit anything beyond 300 paces, while the Allies reached them at 1,200 paces and more. When they got near enough to equalize the disadvantages in range, their battalions were disorganized by the allied fire."

Serving in the trenches with the 90th Regiment was Lieutenant Garnet Wolseley who, when not working as a volunteer engineering officer, engaged in sharpshooting. He would wait by a loophole with a cocked rifle and have an enlisted man raise a forage cap on a ramrod just slightly over the parapet. The moment a Russian fired and revealed his position, Wolseley fired at the smoke. Afterwards, if the Russians commenced an artillery bombardment, it convinced Wolseley that he had either killed or wounded a Russian. After one shot, the bombardment was so horrific, that the officer of the day investigated and after learning that Wolseley was responsible, ordered him "to shut up." Wolseley desisted for only a while before he began sharpshooting Russian gunners or any other man who exposed himself. In a letter to his dowager aunt, he explained, "man shooting is the finest sport of all, there is a certain amount of infatuation about it, the more you kill the more you wish to kill."

Among the 1/95 was Lieutenant Godfrey, who "proceeding in advance of his battalion with a few men, under the cover of a ridge, made such excellent shooting at the Russian gunners (at 600 yards) the men handing him their rifles as fast as he fired that, in his own words, 'We got the credit of silencing them.'" Godfrey's feat was substantiated by Todleben who wrote that "… the enormous losses which the enemy's riflemen inflicted on the Russian Artillery. A perfect cloud of riflemen, hid in thick brushwood, opened a very accurate fire against our artillery at a distance of 800 paces. Some of our guns from time to time rained case on them, but the discharge only checked the fire of the enemy's riflemen for a minute. … It was more the fire of rifled small arms than that of the artillery of the enemy which reached our artillerymen, of which the greater part were killed or wounded."

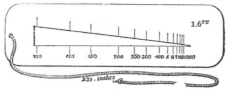
Stadium.

Teleometer.

Wanting its own sharpshooter battalion, the British 1st Division instructed each battalion to detach one non-commissioned officer and ten men to form an ad hoc sharpshooter battalion. Commanded by Captain Gerald Goodlake, the tiny battalion was guarding the left flank when it was approached by a 600-strong Russian column. They killed numerous Russians in their fighting retreat with Goodlake alone killing five men. One man he shot through the head at 300 yards. As effective as they were, losses in the parent battalions meant the men could no longer be detailed and Goodlake's battalion was disbanded after only two months of service.

One month later General Conrobert decided that a position known as the Ovens needed to be captured. From this position the Russian sharpshooters enfiladed the French batteries and harassed the British sappers. The Allies attacked and captured the position. Among the casualties was Lieutenant Henry Tyron, 1/95, who, in the course of the campaign, killed at least 100 Russians with 30 being killed in one day alone. Tyron had emptied his revolver at close quarters and was conspicuously standing while reloading a rifle when he was killed.

The Russians were not without their own riflemen and Colonel Reynell Pack, 7th Fusiliers, recalled losing two men to one Russian sharpshooter:

> Through one of the sand-bag loop-holes a British private had been firing with, as he fancied, indifferent success, and therefore took a sergeant into consultation; the latter was judging the distance and looking through the loop-hole, whilst the private, much interested,

looked over the sergeant's shoulder. Nothing could be seen of these two men above the parapets, except perhaps the moving of their forage caps, but so judicious was the judgment and so excellent the aim of a Russian rifleman, that a shot entered the loop-hole, passed through the head of the sergeant and the throat of the private, killing both men. As the small loop-hole was scarcely visible such a shot could only have been made by the marksman calculating where the face was from the slight circumstance of a cap being observed an inch or two over the parapet, breaking the regularity of the line of defense. The two poor victims to such deadly aim were buried on the spot where they fell, and their arms and accoutrements carried back to camp.

The Indian Mutiny

The Indian Mutiny in 1857 provided another opportunity for the minié gun to show its potential. At the siege of Delhi, two Indian buglers were simultaneously shot at long range by two British riflemen. An unidentified Indian marksman nicknamed Jim the Nailer by the British was known for picking off any soldier who carelessly exposed himself. At Cawnpore Captain Atherly, 3/95, asked Rifleman Robertson to estimate the distance to a brick kiln. Robertson replied that he didn't know, but brought Atherly's attention to a man standing adjacent to it. Atherly adjusted his sights and shot the man through the stomach at 600 yards distance.

An interesting incident occurred involving the Black Watch (42nd Highlanders) at Secundrabah:

> When the slaughter in the Secundrabah was almost over, many of the soldiers lay down under a large peepul tree with a very bushy top, to enjoy its shade and quench their thirst from the jars of cool water set around the foot of the tree. An exceptional number of dead and wounded also lay under the tree, and this attracted the notice of an officer. Carefully examining the wounds, he found that

Single-shot v. Repeaters. The quest for increased firepower was attempted in numerous ways. Multiple barrels resulted in a heavier than normal firearm. Another is to have multiple chambers, as in a revolving cylinder. These however were difficult to manufacture. A third was to load the barrel like a roman candle and have a sliding lock for each touchhole. This was proposed to the Continental Congress but no surviving examples are known. Perhaps the most innovative was the Lorenzoni rotating breechblock. Tipped downward, a cylindrical breechblock operated by a large handle was rotated away from the user to deposit powder into the breechblock and then a ball. When the handle was rotated toward the user, the ball was deposited into the barrel, and then the powder, and finally the frizzen was snapped shut and ready to fire. Safety depended on how finely machined the cylinder was with respects to the magazine. A worn cylinder meant a spark could enter the magazine. All these designs were difficult and expensive to make and it was easier to equip an army with single-shots firearms.

Repeaters were finally made practical with the introduction of the metallic cartridge, allowing for magazines integral to the firearm which, when combined with breechloading, made repeaters safe from gas leakage. When fired, the metallic cartridge would expand, sealing the breech and preventing and gas leakage toward the user. One early design was the Volcanic Arms lever action pistol which later evolved into the Henry lever action rifle of the American Civil War. Repeaters gave the infantryman to hold off many times his number and were successfully used in the Civil War and later in the Russo-Turkish battle at Plevna (1877).

Henry Heth.

in every case the men had evidently been shot from above. The officer called to a soldier to look if he could see anyone in the tree-top. The soldier had his rifle loaded, and stepping back, he carefully scanned the top of the tree. He almost immediately called out: "I see him sir!" Cocking his rifle, he immediately fired, and down fell a body dressed in a tight-fitting red jacket and tight-fitting rose-coloured silk trousers; and the breast of the jacket bursting open with the fall, showed that the wearer was a woman. She was armed with a pair of heavy old-pattern cavalry pistols, one of which was in her belt still loaded, and her pouch was still half full of ammunition. From her perch in the tree, which had been carefully prepared before the attack, she had killed more than a dozen men.

* * *

Within a short period what had once been considered an extraordinary shot became easily attainable. For the first time a common infantryman could be equipped with a weapon that was accurate out to 500 yards without compromising on the volume of fire thought to win battles. The 1850s saw a proliferation of bullet designs based on variations of Captain Minié's bullet. In America, the United States Army adopted its own minié rifle, the 1855 Springfield rifle musket. Having the technology and being able to take advantage of it was another matter. In the antebellum era Winfield Hancock sent Henry Heth an *Illustrated London News* clipping that briefly described the Hythe school's rifle instruction. Using it, Heth trained his men and reported his observations, which were plagiarized and published by another officer.

Since the effective combat range could be extended, two schools of thought emerged in Europe—one contending that armies would never again approach to within close proximity of each other since long-range fire would make casualties too high, and the other asserting that the bayonet would still decide the battle. The Second Italian War of Independence (1859) decided the issue in favor of the bayonet for the Americans.

Muzzleloaders v Breechloaders. Until the mid-19th century, muzzleloaders dominated the firearms world. They required the user to pour powder, wadding and ball down the barrel from the muzzle to load it. Generally but not always the muzzle was held upright, making the user dangerously exposed during the loading process. Early attempts at loading from the breech included a breechloading pistol and shield made for Henry VIII's personal bodyguards. Breechloading required removal of the breechblock or some sort of a plug. This allowed the user to insert the ball and then powder from the rear of the barrel. Replacing the breechblock, the user was ready to shoot. Breechloading was faster and minimized the user's exposure. The main problem with breechloading is that it required precise hand fitting to ensure that no gases escaped from the breech when the firearm was discharged. Being labor intensive, this was not cost effective until the Industrial Revolution and the advent of machinery.

CHAPTER 4

THE AMERICAN CIVIL WAR

1861–65

*"Man is the noblest game after all; no other chase compares for a
moment with the hunting of human lives. Sharpshooters … will tell
you that lion hunting is nothing to it. … Of all the pleasures I can
imagine none more exciting than to bring down your man at long
range. Of course this is a serious game, yet there is nothing to be said
against it if you are both patriot and marksman. For in that case you
get the highest pleasure and the highest duty in one. To lie behind a
stump, a heavy rifle in your hand, and the enemy within reach, and
then to pick him off skillfully."*

Titus Munson Coan

THE TERM "SHARPSHOOTER" AS USED BY the Civil War soldier
is almost interchangeable with skirmisher and in reading any
Civil War memoir, diary or journal the reader should not assume
that sharpshooter is synonymous with sniper. During the Civil
War, two types of sharpshooters emerged. The vast majority were
men who specialized as skirmishers and who fought in a manner
much like the 5/60, Rifle Brigade, and other light infantry. The
second were the specialized riflemen who fought independently
and chose their own ground. These men carried target rifles or
rifles that were more accurate than the standard infantry rifle.

Selecting and training sharpshooters

At war's outbreak, Yankee inventor and expert rifle shot Hiram Berdan proposed raising a regiment of sharpshooters to the War Department. As envisioned by Berdan, sharpshooters would never fight in the line of battle, join in a charge, need a bayonet, or stand picket. Instead they would be fighting from afar, carefully selecting their targets and removing them. Armed with a breechloading double set trigger Sharps rifle, they were to be the Union's snipers—or so Berdan thought. Calls went out and only men who could satisfy the War Department's requirement would be accepted into the service. These men were to "at a distance of 200 yards, at a rest, put ten consecutive shots into a target, the average distance not to exceed five inches from the center of the Bull's eye to the center of the ball." The response was so enthusiastic that not one but two regiments were raised with a third contemplated. Besides Berdan's two regiments, there were numerous formally raised battalions like the 1st Battalion New York Sharpshooters, 1st Maine Sharpshooter Battalion, a battalion from Ohio as well as numerous independent companies that were attached to various regiments.

The First Michigan Sharpshooters lacked volunteers and used draftees to fill its ranks. This required some men to receive

---

Some muzzleloading guns were equipped with **two triggers**. Applying pressure on the rear trigger prepared the forward or "set" trigger to be used. The "set" trigger was very light and can be adjusted in most cases, to a matter of mere ounces such that the slightest touch would discharge the firearm.

Sharps rifle carried by Berdan's Sharpshooters. (Gettysburg Collection)

marksmanship instruction before qualifying as sharpshooters and the training must have been effective since almost everyone passed.

It is unknown whether Birge's Western Sharpshooters (66th Illinois Volunteer Infantry) were required to qualify. Raised by General Charles Fremont, no evidence has been found to suggest that they did. We know from accounts at Fort Donelson that they conducted themselves much like Berdan's Sharpshooters and were initially armed with civilian hunting or target rifles.

Initially the Confederacy did not raise sharpshooters, that need was filled by a regiment's flank companies. This practice dates to the Colonial era when Companies A and J, the light infantry and grenadier companies of a regiment, were detailed for skirmishing. It would not be until April 1862 that the Confederate Congress authorized the raising of sharpshooter battalions. The only specification made by the Confederate Congress was that battalions were composed of select men. Select was defined neither by Congress nor the adjutant general. Who selected them and the criteria for their selection was open to interpretation. This resulted in multiple methods used by the Confederates to raise sharpshooters.

Since a company was generally a reflection of the community from which it was raised, and the men knew each other as classmates, coworkers, neighbors, church parishioners, friends, relatives, etc., they were loathe to part it for a company of strangers. As a solution, some companies were transferred regardless of the quality of its personnel. Similarly entire units were converted, like the 30th Virginia Artillery which became the 30th Battalion Virginia Sharpshooters. Draftees were inducted whether or not the draftee had any aptitude as a soldier or marksmanship skills. Some units allowed the men to vote on who transferred. Another method was for the officers to select disliked, troublesome, or sickly soldiers. In a few cases and before the practice was discontinued, men took up a subscription and hired a substitute for the sharpshooter battalion. The final and best method was to screen volunteers. Generally the candidate had to be a marksman, battle proven, and have fidelity to the cause.

Inconsistency in selection meant that the Confederate sharpshooter of 1862 was no better than his line infantryman counterpart. This did not matter to most officers since sharp-shooting meant skirmishing and that was just another onerous task that any infantryman could perform. Inasmuch as the Union brigade-level officer did not understand how to optimize the sharpshooter, their Confederate counterparts were equally ignorant and officers on both sides were still learning their trade as soldiers. There were exceptions though and in the Army of Northern Virginia, Robert Rodes' and William Wofford's battalions were composed of men who were carefully selected.

In the Confederate Army of Tennessee, battalions were raised by transferring entire companies into new sharpshooter battalions. No evidence has been found showing they received any specialized marksmanship training. The exception was Major General Patrick R. Cleburne's division. A veteran of the 41st Welch Regiment, Cleburne had a copy of the British musketry manual and used its methodology to train his division. He took a special interest in sharpshooting and raised his small company of sharpshooters before the Confederate Adjutant General issued the order. The father of the Confederate sharpshooter, Cleburne's division's reputation for marksmanship was recognized by it receiving twenty Whitworth rifles and ten Kerr target rifles—more than any other division.

Upon arrival at their camp of instruction, the Union recruit began drilling under Hardee's Rifle and Light Infantry Tactics (1861). This included marching by squad, platoons, companies, battalions, and regiments. They were also instructed on skirmishing, which called for sending men forward of the line of battle to engage and defeat the enemy's skirmishers, pick off their officers and to dominate the terrain. The difficulty of commanding and controlling a large body of men dispersed over a vast expanse of ground was resolved by using bugle signals. This is described in one sharpshooter's letter:

> So I have been out about two miles from camp on a skirmish and Battalion drill for the first time. I was taken from my own company and put into Co. B, a company that has been here two or three months. So after we had got out into the woods the 2nd and 7th Company in the regiment were sent out as skirmishers to see if we could spy any rebels. Mind you we were on drill, not in the region of rebels. We went out a little way, deployed as skirmishers and went on at double quick. We had not gone far before the order was given to halt just as if we had seen some of the enemy. When the order to halt is given when we are skirmishing we halt and run for the nearest tree and if there is none we lay flat on our bellies so as to get out the reach of the enemy fire.

Other than the 1st Michigan Sharpshooters, no evidence has been found to support that the marksmanship instructions were provided to Berdan's or other Union sharpshooters. Instead Berdan's Sharpshooters conducted target practice to hone their skills:

> Prize shooting was occasionally allowed, and usually created a healthy excitement among the men, as well as the visitors who were sure to be there. One of the most important of these matches was held on Thanksgiving afternoon (November 28th) between members of the target-rifle companies C, E and F, each man firing two shots off-hand at 40 rods [5.5 yards], the winner to receive $5, presented by the colonel. The day being fine there was a large attendance of public men and others who came from town to "see

the Sharpshooters shoot;" the judges, Capt. Giroux of Company C and Sergt. Stevens of Company G, awarded the prize to a Vermonter named Ai Brown, his shot measuring four and one-quarter inches from the center. H. J. Peck of the same company, a prominent marksman, was a close second in the match—almost a tie.

Sharpshooter training in the Army of Northern Virginia (1863–64) was more systematic and patterned after "American skirmish and French zouave drills and introduced by the commander for the government of a battalion on field, while a 'manual of arms' in the form of a brochure upon the system of rifle training was furnished by Maj. Gen. Wilcox." The latter was most likely based on Appendix B of General Cadmus Wilcox's ante-bellum (1859) treatise:

> As soon as the requisite number of men was obtained, a separate camp was established, and in every respect the command was placed on an independent footing—reporting, in the case of a regiment, directly to brigade headquarters. Thus closely associated together, rank and file soon learned to know and to rely upon each other. Still further to increase this confidence, the companies were subdivided into groups of fours, something like the French army's comrades de bataille. These groups messed and slept together, and were never separated in action, save by its casualties of disability and death. The further strengthening of this body was hoped to be accomplished by thorough drill.

Training included firearms cleaning, disassembly and explanation of every part and its function, the care of the firearm, cartridge box and ammunition, the effects of wind on the bullet, the sun on the sights, shooting uphill or downhill, an explanation of the barrel including rifling, and the diagnosing of misfires. Aiming instructions were also given and as feedback, the guns were mounted onto tripods and sighted by the soldier. His officer would then inspect the sights to check the alignment. If the sighting was defective, he would call upon another soldier who was to point out the error. Afterward the officer offered

Major William Dunlop.

some remarks to the class. After perfecting sight alignment, the soldiers practiced dry firing.

The ability to accurately estimate distances was crucial since it enabled the sharpshooter to adjust his sight, as noted by William Dunlop:

> The battalion was first put on drill in estimating distances. It was drawn up in line in open field; a man or an object the size of a man was stationed in front at an unknown distance, about 100 yards off, and the roll called; at the call of each name the man stepped forward ten paces, surveyed carefully the object in front, calculated the intervening space, and deliberately announced in exact figures his estimate of the distance between, and a record was made of his judgment; then the next in the same way, and so on through the entire command. The distance was increased from time to time, from one hundred to two, three, five and nine hundred yards, and an accurate account kept of each man's judgment in each drill. The practice in this drill was continued from day to day until every man could tell, almost to a mathematical certainty, the distance at any given point within the compass of his drill. A few, however, were naturally and hopelessly deficient in their powers of estimating distance, and hence, were exchanged for others.

This was essentially the same drill taught to Civil War artillery gun layers who had to set the fuse for their shells. Those who were proficient at estimating distances next engaged in target practice:

> The battalion was formed on the range, a target about the size of a man was placed in front at a distance of one hundred yards, with a bullseye in the center of about five inches in diameter enclosed

within an inner circle of about fourteen inches and an outer circle of about twenty-four inches; a tripod was constructed of convenient height, with a sandbag lodged in the fork on which to rest a heavy rifle while the soldier aimed and fired, and the practice began:

The target for 100 yards, pine plank one inch thick, 2 × 6 feet.
The target for 500 yards, pine plank one inch thick, 4 × 6 feet.
The target for 900 yards, pine plank one inch thick, 6 × 6 feet.
The bullseye was enlarged, as well as the circles, as the distance was extended.

The roll was called, as in the first drill, and each man in turn stepped forward to the tripod, aimed and fired; the flag man at the target announced, by signal, the result of the fire, which was recorded; and the practice continued until the entire battalion had taken part in the drill. This practice was continued from day to day, and the distance increased from time to time up to 900 yards, with a complete record kept of each drill, until the results achieved in estimating distance and rifle training were as amazing to the brigade commander as they were gratifying to the officers and men of the battalion.

This drill originated from the British musketry manual which recommended: "the shots that strikes the target are to be denoted by flags of different colours raised above the butt." While useful, the manual was not always followed by the Confederates and in some battalions, the requisite 60 rounds course of fire was not adhered to. "We shot two rounds apiece at the distance of 600 yards. Out of 98 shots, only five hit the board. I was one of the five and I missed the cross some distance." The same sharpshooter described the next day's practice. "I have just returned from our morning's lesson of target shooting. I did about the same as yesterday and missed the board the first shot and hit it the next. There was considerable improvement in the other boys. A good number of shots struck the board. We shot at 600 yards, the same distance as yesterday." Modernly, two shots a day is not much practice at all: the first shot dirties the bore and allows the shooter to adjust his sights or his hold for his next shot.

Sharpshooter on picket duty, Army of the Potomac.

As attrition created vacancies, it is unlikely that the replacements received any of this training since time and opportunity were lacking.

Equipment

Specialized equipment included tree-climbing spikes, as described by Berdan's Sharpshooter Captain Stevens: "Two men in each company were also furnished with 'climbers,' to be used on special occasions in climbing trees." The spikes were flat iron bars 15½ inches long and about 5½ inches wide at the stirrup. A hooked spike was on the end of the stirrup and to use the climbing spike, the sharpshooter stood on the stirrup and secured it to his shoe or boot with a leather strap and another leather strap to secure the top of the climbing spike secure to his leg. No similar example has been found for the Confederates.

Range-finding devices, called stadias, were also available. They came with a piece of string or chain attached. The user held the string or chain beneath the eye socket and held the stadia out as far

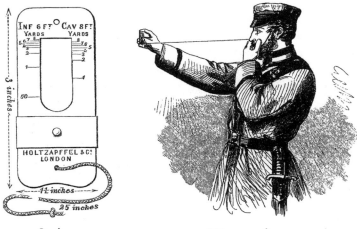

Stadium.   *Using a stadium*

as the string or chain extended. He then fitted the object into the graduated slot and looked at the number to calculate the distance.

By necessity the cheek must be placed against the rifle's comb to aim and in trench warfare, the slightest exposure invited a bullet. This was especially dangerous when exposing oneself in a loophole or peering out from behind a log. How the danger was eliminated is described by one soldier:

> Now we would get a small stick, sharpen one end of it and slit the other end and put a small tin case looking-glass in the split (most of the boys carried them) and sit with our backs toward the Rebels and our guns stuck in the holes behind us, the muzzles pointed toward the Rebels … the guns cocked and our thumbs on the triggers. We would take the stick with the looking-glass in it and stick it in the bank front of us and whenever anything came across the gun to the glass we would pull the trigger.

By 1864, the concept was refined: "The Yankees would hold up small looking glasses, so that our strength and breastworks could be seen in the reflection in the glass; and they also had small mirrors on the butts of their guns, so arranged that they could sight up the barrels of their guns by looking through these glasses, while they themselves would not be exposed to our fire, and they kept up this continual firing day and night, whether they could see us or not." One Union officer described it further: "There was a Yankee who came to me and showed me a small looking glass about one inch square attached to a wire that was inserted into a hole bored near the breech of a musket. Lay the musket over the works, cock the gun, looking into the glass, and when you see ahead, fire. We found we had the right thing in the right place … by using those glasses on the guns we were able to keep them from doing us any harm." This did little to repair their broken bonds of affection and the mystic chords of memory with their Confederate counterparts.

While some Confederates were aware that mirrors were used for aiming safely, the only thing Confederates used them for was for observation:

> The following incident will convey some idea of the precision of marksmanship attained by constant practice. It was told me repeatedly by Isaac Newman, one of the most fearless and truthful men I ever knew. He was the survivor of the episode. Newman and a comrade, whose name was Blake, I think, were detailed as sharpshooters in one of the rifle-pits in our front. Sharpshooters were posted and relieved at night, and but once in twenty-four hours. The attempt to reach or return from a rifle-pit in the daytime would have been followed by certain death. The pit was a hole in the ground large enough to contain two men. A curtain of earth was thrown up in front, with a narrow embrasure through which to fire. On the inside was a small banquette in front, upon which the men could sit or kneel when firing. Newman and Blake were reckless and resourceful chaps. They hit upon the device of taking a small looking-glass into the pit with them. This they hung opposite the embrasure. By this arrangement they could sit on the banquette, with their backs to the enemy, and see in the looking glass all that was going on in front, without exposing their heads.

Realizing that shooting straight at a target invited return fire, one Confederate devised a box for oblique shooting:

> … so constructed and arraigned on the parapet, as it would give protection to the sharpshooters. He constructed one … 4 feet long, 6 to 8 inches square, its ends sawed off diagonally, this was placed on the parapet, at an angle of 45 degrees, sand-bags placed in front, to hide it from view of the enemy and protect the sharpshooter. Its test proved satisfactory, the sharpshooter had an opportunity, to get a fair sight of the Federal soldier, his aim was accurate, he fired, the smoke instead of issuing from his front, was seen issuing from our lines, from a point 2 or 3 feet to his right or left, the Federal sharpshooters, would naturally aim at this point without inflicting any damage to the Confederate soldier …

Field craft

While camouflage clothing was not invented yet, the advantage of concealment was understood and it was not without reason that German *jägers* and British riflemen wore green. Similarly green was selected by Berdan for the regimental uniform. Other sharpshooter units were not so fortunate and were issued the same uniform issued to other infantry and this included the 1st Battalion New York Sharpshooters whose sole concession was to have black rubber buttons instead of brass ones. Some had the blue uniform but trimmed with green to signify their "sharpshooter" status. While unintentional, the gray or butternut worn by the Confederates also delivered similar results, as will be discussed later.

Field-expedient camouflage was practiced particularly by the Indians who applied their field craft and shared it. Colonel Charles DeLand, commanding officer of the 1st Michigan Sharpshooters, remembered the Indians of Company K teaching the rest of the regiment:

They, on the very first day at the front, caught on to the great advantage our enemy employed over us in the color of uniform. Ours was blue and could be seen at a long distance; while the "Johnny" (as we called them) could not be spotted at comparatively short distance, even when lying in an open field. This disadvantage to us was appreciated almost immediately that these Indians got in the field, and they would go out and find a dry spot of earth and roll in it until their uniform was the complete color of the ground before going out in the skirmish line; and if the day was wet, they would not hesitate to take mud and rub it over their clothes, for as soon as this dried a little would have what they were after the color of earth. This custom was adopted by my whole Regiment; and it was often remarked that our Regiment could do the closest skirmishing at the least cost of any Regiment in the Division.

A chance meeting made one sharpshooter the pupil of one Indian. White had been ordered to annoy the Confederate artillery and needed to cross a cornfield, across some open terrain to get to some brush where he could conceal himself:

> I was very sure that if I tried to cross the opening that the rebel pickets would get a bullet into me. While on the ridge I met a Michigan soldier and he was under the same orders I was. He was a full blooded Indian. I told him that I wished that I could get down to the cover of brush but the corn was not large or thick enough to cover us from the view of the rebels. The Indian said, "Make self corn. Do as I do." He then cut off the stalks of corn and began to stick them into his clothes and equipment. I did as he did and then we worked our way to the fence and cover of bushes without even drawing rebel fire.

Post-Napoleonic War experiments by the British Army showed that light gray was the least visible of all colors and that it blended well with the white smoke that followed a gun's discharge. It also was excellent for towns and at Gettysburg fifteen-year-old Tillie Pierce Alleman remarked that the Confederates were "a filthy, dirty-looking set." Her father hushed her by pointing out a nearby Confederate who had knelt to tie his shoelaces. "Oh my," Tillie replied, "I didn't see him! They were actually so much the color of the street, that it was no wonder we failed to notice this one." One Union private commented on the Confederates. "They were covered with filthy rags and represented all colors of a Virginia landscape, red mud being the predominant tint. I have often wondered why we can't see the Rebels better; now I have the answer. If this lot of Rebels had been lying on the ground we could have passed very near them and not suspected their presence, mistaking them for rocks, logs, and dirt."

The aforementioned were incidental examples of how the Confederate gray or butternut blended well with the terrain. However, there is evidence of intended camouflage too: "The enemy skulked behind every hiding place, and sought relief in the oak leaves, between which their uniforms that there was so strong a resemblance, our men were continually deceived by them." Other Confederate sharpshooters made efforts to conceal themselves, "We have frequently resorted to various artifices in our warfare. Sometimes we would climb a tree and pin leaves all over our clothes to keep their color from betraying us."

Sharpshooter Edom Moon described how his squad camouflaged their position and then lured some United States Colored Troops into the open under the pretense of bartering. Instead of bartering, they ambushed the hapless men. Camouflage was also used for stalking and Union Major Joseph Stockton describes it:

> I was much interested today in watching a number of Indians that belong to the 14th Wisconsin acting as sharpshooters. … These Indians had fixed their heads with leaves in such a way that you could not tell them. They would creep on their bellies a little distance, then keep quiet, then move ahead until they could get the position they were after, which was generally a log, behind which they could lie without very much exposure. They silenced the rebel cannon in front [of our position] almost entirely.

Tactics

Sharpshooting was more than shooting accurately. It also required guile to induce the opponent to reveal their location. The most convenient ruse was to place one's hat on a ramrod and move it slightly to entice the opponent to shoot. When he did, the return fire would dispatch him. This of course required teamwork with one sharpshooter offering the bait and the other lying in wait. A Berdan's Sharpshooter describes the ruse:

> Locating the enemy's position, four of our Sharpshooters deployed, two on each side of the road, and advance carefully through the brush some 200 yards where they lay quietly watching for further developments; but seeing or hearing nothing they rigged up a stick with a hat and coat, and shoved it out across the roadway, when instantly a report was heard and a bullet crashed through the coat. The puff of smoke seeming to issue from the center of a tree 100 yards distant, the Sharpshooters then crawled forward to either side of the road, keeping under cover as much as possible, firing at the right and left side of the tree, the result being of a very damaging character to the concealed Johnny, the receiving his quietus.

Dummies were also used to draw fire and one Union soldier recalled being deceived: "One day I and two of my companions fired for an hour at a rebel who kept forever hopping up and down behind the sand bags and calling constantly, 'Try again, will you, Mr. Yankee?' Finally the figure mounted up in full view, when we discovered we were cheaply sold, as the daring rebel was a stuffed suit of old clothes on a pole, while the mockery came from the real rebel, safe behind the sand bags." It was fortunate that the Confederate did not arrange for any of his comrades to lay in wait for the Yankees to expose themselves to shoot.

After Gettysburg was captured, the Confederates occupied the town and the sharpshooters went to work in the attics of several houses. By removing some bricks, they created loopholes from which they shot the defenders of Culp's Hill. The Yankees fought back the best they could, but couldn't do what was necessary—drive the Confederates out with artillery, since there was a possibility that civilians could still be in Gettysburg. The Confederates relented only when they evacuated Gettysburg.

Because of their height, trees offered an excellent observation post from which to observe the enemy's movement. Trees were used during the American Revolution as well as the Indian Mutiny. The danger of using a tree was that once detected, there was no cover to speak of and the sharpshooter was extremely vulnerable. In recognition of this danger, one Confederate officer whose men carried either Whitworth or Kerr target rifles expressly forbade his men from using trees. The men and rifles were too valuable to risk losing.

Much safer was a tower-like structure built by the Confederates on the Wilderness battlefield. "The high parapet was not only traversed as often as every ten or twelve feet, but was enclosed on the rear, so that the line was divided into a series of spare pens, with the banks of earth heavily riveted with oak logs. From space to space was what looked like a wooden camp chimney. But in truth was an elevated post for sharpshooters with a little loophole in front." During the Union siege of Vicksburg, a Lincoln log tower was built by Lieutenant Henry C. Foster. Known in XVII Corps as "Coonskin" for his coonskin cap, Foster was reputed to be the best shot in the army. As the Confederate artillery had been silenced, there was no fear of the tower being shot down. Besides shooting from it, mirrors were mounted to enable the Union mortar men to drop their shells into the Confederate trenches. Naturally the Confederates shot out the mirrors but they were replaced nightly. Ordered to silence the Rebel sharpshooters, Foster "went out once at night-time, crept up toward the Confederate defenses and built himself a burrow in the ground, with a peep hole in it. There he would frequently take provisions with him and stay several days at a time, watching for the Confederates."

Rifles

Many recruited into Berdan's Sharpshooters had been allured by a promise that they would have telescope-equipped Sharps breechloading rifles. The Ordnance Department didn't have any available and offered Berdan the Springfield rifle musket. First, scopes were not mass produced and in America were individually hand made. Second, having Sharps shut down the carbine line to produce rifles would not only slow down the delivery of carbines for the cavalry, but result in a lull in production while the line was converted over to produce rifles.

Another recruitment promise was that every man who brought his own target rifle would be compensated for it. As this promise was never made by the War Department but by the officers who recruited them, it was never fulfilled. However, two companies (and part of a third company, C, D, and E) of Berdan's First United States Sharpshooters marched off to war armed with target rifles. Two other companies from Massachusetts were supposed to join Berdan's regiments, but Massachusetts Governor Andrew intervened and decided that they should fight alongside Massachusetts men. Named after their governor, they were known as the 1st and 2nd Andrew's Sharpshooters.

Since neither target rifle nor Sharps breechloaders were available, Army Ordnance Chief Ripley offered Berdan the common Springfield rifle musket. Seeking to keep logistics simple, Ripley was unreceptive to firearms innovation. Doing so would create a logistical nightmare with various types of ammunition as well as spare parts for repair. Berdan knew that the men would reject the Springfield and declined them. Berdan wrote to General-in-Chief McClellan asking for the .56 caliber Colt Root Revolving Rifle, a five-shot rifle that had a revolving cylinder much like modern revolvers. Berdan's letter eventually reached President Lincoln who overrode Ripley's objection.

While the Root Revolving Rifle offered the advantage of being a repeater, it was generally disliked by the men who reluctantly accepted them only on the premise that it was an interim arm

Morgan James scoped rifle with false muzzle. (West Point Collection)

until the Sharps could be supplied. There were several complaints but it was chiefly related to a revolver's habit of spitting lead shavings out from between the gap of the cylinder mouth and the barrel. The lead shavings "fly six to eight feet endangering a persons eyes." Men picked lead from each other's face and neck. More dangerously the design was not immune from multiple cylinders discharging simultaneously. Called chain fires, they are attributable to loosely fitting percussion caps that moved when the gun discharged. The danger is that if the sharpshooter held onto the forearm, he could end up with lead balls embedded in him, as was the case for one sharpshooter whose hand was disfigured by a chain fire.

Eventually the .52 caliber Sharps breechloading rifle was issued to the Berdan Sharpshooters and they gladly exchanged their Colts for the Sharps. The falling block Sharps had been adopted by the cavalry before the war and was perhaps the best breechloader in service. Breechloaders have been around since Henry VIII but they all suffered from inadequate gas sealing. The result was dangerous hot gases near the user's face—something neither conducive to marksmanship nor user confidence in his firearm. The Sharps overcame this problem with a two-piece gas seal. Within the sliding breechblock was Conant gas check and the Lawrence cylindrical insert. Upon firing, the gases blew the Conant gas check against the Lawrence cylindrical insert. When the gas check and cylindrical insert were pressed against each other, they prevented any gas from escaping. Being a breechloader they were easier to clean than a muzzle-loader and easier to reload while prone. Weighing

Born in Ostego, New York, **Truman Head** headed west to California where he engaged in various pursuits including grizzly hunting. At war's outbreak, he joined Company C. of Berdan's Sharpshooters and privately purchased a Sharps breechloading rifle. Being one of the oldest members of the regiment, he acquired the moniker California Joe, and was a regimental favorite. Besides the Sharps, there are numerous accounts of him using a scoped rifle with which he killed a Negro rebel sharpshooter. After Malvern Hill, Head was hospitalized for vision problems and discharged on November 3, 1862. He returned to San Francisco where he worked as a laborer and a night inspector for the U.S. Customs Department. He passed away in 1875 and is interred at the Presidio National Cemetery in San Francisco under his given name.

Hiram Berdan and California Joe

only 8 pounds, the Sharps was lighter than the Springfield and its shorter 30-inch barrel was much handier than the longer 39-inch barrel Springfield.

The Sharps was carried by Berdan's men throughout the course of the war and was not exclusive to them. Other infantry units known to be partially equipped with Sharps include the New York Independent Sharpshooters and both companies of Andrew's Sharpshooters.

The Confederates were at a disadvantage in having less industrial capacity, and relied on Enfield rifles for their sharpshooters. A single-shot rifle musket, the Enfield was the English equivalent to the American Springfield. Whereas the Springfield was capable of hitting a man at 500 yards, the Enfield could be relied on up to 900 yards. Firing a bullet slightly smaller than the Springfield's, its accuracy was attributable to the progressive depth rifling. Most Enfields imported during the war had a 39-inch-long barrel and among the Confederates the shorter 33-inch rifle was reserved for the Confederate sharpshooters.

During the war, both sides issued non-standardized firearms in limited numbers. On the Union side, Horace E. Dimick of St. Louis, Missouri was contracted to provide target rifles for Birge's Western Sharpshooters. Dimick came from Kentucky and in 1849 opened shop on 38 North Main Street. While competing with the Hawkens Brothers, Dimick's line also included target rifles. As a private maker, there was no set pattern or caliber and each rifle could be distinct from the next. They had either brass or steel hardware (trigger guard, buttplate, thimbles escutcheon for lock screws, nose). Some had poured pewter noses. Generally they are similar in appearance to the Hawkens (sometimes misspelled as Hawkins) rifles carried by many Fur Trade-era trappers. The half-stocked ones had a metal rib beneath the barrel. The nose served to protect foreend wood as well as being the entry pipe for the ramrod. Some had the sharp crescent-shaped buttplate which were intended to be shot off the arm and not the shoulder. The trigger guards varied, depending on what was available to the maker. Double set triggers were also optional on these guns. Since Dimick catered to the civilian market, there was no fixed caliber, and surviving examples have been found in .34, .48, and .50 caliber with barrel lengths varying from 31 to 36 inches. Since each rifle bore was a unique caliber, the rifle was accompanied by a bullet mold with which the user could cast bullets.

Whether the rifle was made by the Hawkens or Dimick, these rifles had very heavy barrels that were designed to withstand a heavy (100 grains FF) powder charge. When he received the contract, Dimick had only about 150 rifles at hand. To meet his contractual obligation, Dimick bought rifles from other makers including Eastern gunsmiths. The December 1862 Illinois Adjutant General Report states, "The regiment is all armed with the sporting rifle." By the 1863 second quarter report there were only 538 remaining and by the 1864 fourth quarter report, this

---

Blackpowder is available in various grain size and from coarser to finer grain they are in the following sequence: F, 2F (or FF), 3F (FFF) and 4F (FFFF). F would be used in very large bore punt guns, 2F for muskets and some rifles (from .72 to .50), 3F for revolvers and some rifles (.50 cal. down to .30 cal.) and 4F for priming flintlock pans. Measurement of powder is by volume and not by weight. Soldiers carried paper cartridges that had a premeasured powder charge. Most Civil War-era muskets and minié guns had about 60–65 grains of 2F. .45 caliber round balls are about 40 grains of 2F. In working up a load for the maximum accuracy, sportsmen often experiment with different powder charges and bullet design or in the case of patched round ball, ball diameter and patch thickness.

had dropped to thirteen. Their duties as skirmishers created a demand for greater firepower and many men bought Henry lever action repeaters.

Target rifles were used in limited numbers by both sides. There is no common characteristic of a target rifle and some were slightly heavier than a regular rifle musket while others were 50 pounds! The optically equipped ones were known in the vernacular of the period as target telescope rifles. Besides bullet molds and bullet swagers to size them, some also had patch cutters, false muzzles to protect the muzzle while it was being loaded and bullet starters to start the bullet down the bore. The loss of any of these accouterments meant that the rifle was useless. At Malvern Hill, the knapsacks belonging to the 2nd Andrew's Sharpshooters were stolen meaning that their rifles had to be sent home and Sharps distributed as replacements.

Telescopes are centuries old and the earliest known scoped rifle in America was made in 1776 for Charles Wilson Peale. A portrait painter, Peale was no rifleman and having no understanding of cheek weld, was struck in his eye when it recoiled. As a remedy, a spring-loaded sliding buttpad like the one made in 1770 by English gunmaker Charles Byrne was installed. A militia officer, it is very unlikely Peale's rifle was fired in combat. Scopes became popular around 1830 and the first known use in combat was by Horatio Ross who used a scoped rifle to protect women and children from mutinous sepoys in India (1856).

In 1854, Commander-in-Chief of the British Army Lord Hardinge wanted the best rifle possible for the army. Hardinge specified that the bullet should weigh the same as the service bullet, then 530 grains, but that it could be smaller bore than the .577 currently in use. The only other restriction was that the service charge of 70 grains was used. Accepting the challenge was Joseph Whitworth who was no gunmaker but the finest mechanic of his time. Whitworth believed that a bullet fitted precisely to the bore would yield the greatest accuracy possible. He conducted tests and concluded that a hexagonal bullet fired from a 1:20-inch twist polygonal rifling barrel would yield the best results. Tested in 1857 against the Enfield service rifle, it outshot the Enfield after 500 yards. The Enfield was shooting so wildly at 1,400 yards that it ceased to be tested. The Whitworth on the other hand was capable of striking a 2-foot by 32-foot oak target at 1,880 yards! The bullet not only hit the target but drove deeply into the wood. Easily the most accurate rifle of its time (until surpassed by the Gibbs-Metford rifle), Whitworth failed

During the American Civil War, two types of **lever action repeaters** were fielded by the Union Army. The Spencer required the shooter to put the hammer on half cock, work the lever to eject the spent cartridge and chamber a fresh cartridge, cock it to full cock before shooting it. To reload the Spencer, the soldier removed the magazine tube from the butt and inserted seven rounds before replacing the magazine tube. To facilitate this, a Blakeslee Box that had tin tubes pre-loaded with seven rounds made reloading very quick for the Spencer armed soldier. The Henry was more advanced in that all the soldier had to do was to work the lever. This not only ejected the spent cartridge, it cocked the hammer and reloaded the chamber with a fresh cartridge. Disadvantages include its open, tubular magazine which soldiers had to be mindful to prevent mud or dirt from entering the magazine tube. Second, the Henry's 44 Henry rimfire bullet not as powerful as the .56 caliber Spencer bullet. Armed with either, the Union soldier enjoyed firepower unrivaled by anything produced by the Confederacy.

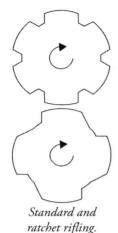

Standard and ratchet rifling.

to gain the military contract since its smaller bore fouled easier than the Enfield and was near impossible to reload when it fouled. Additionally the Whitworth cost four times an Enfield.

An assortment of sights was offered with the Whitworth, but some were also adapted for the side-mounted Davidson scope. Scopes of the period offered limited internal elevation capability. By mounting the scope on the side, the scope could be depressed for distances greater than a centerline barrel-mounted scope. Another advantage of the Davidson side-mounted system was the user could still use his metallic sights. Weighing slightly more than the Enfield, the Whitworth was capable of outshooting a 50-pound target rifle and was highly coveted among the Confederates who competed in shooting matches for the honor of using it. Each Whitworth rifle, along with a bullet mould and 1,000 rounds of ammunition, cost the Confederacy $1,000 in gold.

The Whitworth was not the only coveted English rifle. England in the 1850s was a nation obsessed with long-range shooting. The London Armoury Company produced the Kerr rifle which featured a six-groove ratchet gain twist rifling. Designed by the armoury's superintendent, James Kerr, the twist started slowly and then at about the halfway point it reached its maximum twist which it maintained up to the muzzle. The theory was that the slower twist caused less bullet deformation. Using a powder charge from 2¾ drams (75.2 grains) to 3 drams (82.03 grains) of fine powder, the Kerr fired a .442-inch diameter bullet that weighed 530 grains and was deadly at a mile. Like the Whitworth, the Kerr fouled easily and required swabbing out after every fourth or fifth shot.

Military firearms are designed to withstand field use. In contrast, **target rifles** require special attentiveness by the user to ensure their reliability. Being of a non-military caliber, they likely had set triggers and special sights, if not target telescopes (as scopes were called in the 19th century), their own bullet mould with which the user would "run" or cast their bullets. They could also have patch cutters, bullet swagers to size the bullet, false muzzles to load the gun without damage to the muzzle, bullet starters to start the bullet down the muzzle and a special carrying case to house the target rifle and its accoutrements when not in use. They could also weigh substantially more than a standard soldier's rifle musket varying from 12 pounds to over 50 lb. The heavier rifles required wagon transport and if the wagon broke (one belonging to the 1st Andrew's Sharpshooters did), the sharpshooter was essentially unarmed. Unable to take a bayonet, they were ill suited for close-range fighting.

Battles

After First Manassas (July 1861), the notion that the war would be over after one quick and relatively bloodless battle was forgotten. Command of the Union army now fell to Major General George McClellan. McClellan bypassed the Confederates by having his army transported by ships to Fortress Monroe on Virginia's Yorktown peninsula. They marched up the peninsula until they reached the Confederate fortification at Yorktown. Many in both armies were still armed with smoothbore muskets and this was especially disadvantageous to the Confederates. Eschewing the unnecessary bloodshed, McClellan laid siege instead of storming Yorktown. Here the sharpshooters proved themselves. One Union soldier found himself under fire:

Along our line of intrenchments it was unsafe to expose the person for an instant. I had a practical illustration of this one day when in charge of a fatigue party in the trenches. I stood for a moment in "the open," and a bullet whizzed close to my head. I failed to comprehend its significance, but when another leaden messenger seemed to pass me closer, and I heard its contact with a tree just beyond me, it dawned upon my mind that I was the target for a rebel sharpshooter. I soon spied an object beyond the chimney of a house across the field, distant about four hundred yards. I satisfied myself that a "Johnny" was behind the chimney on the roof, and then sent a message to Col. Berdan, whose sharpshooters were endeavoring to protect us from just such fellows as this one proved to be. Two of Berdan's experts responded to my summons and they began a ceaseless vigil with the purpose of killing or disabling the daring rifleman behind the chimney. They finally prepared an effigy and advanced it to the open plot where I had been exposed, and immediately a head was revealed from behind the chimney, and a rifle bullet sped across the field. We heard its "zip" as it passed the effigy, and then we knew what before we had only surmised. The rebel behind the chimney was determined to slay anyone who came within the range of his rifle. Little suspecting that he had been detected, he again thrust his head from concealment for another shot, but before he had time to bring his rifle into position, a bullet from a Berdan sharpshooter had passed through the intervening space and we saw a human body roll down the shingled roof to the ground.

Civil War muzzle-loading artillery required artillerymen to expose themselves to load. For a brief moment in time the rifleman could challenge and even dominate the artillery. One Union captain watched Berdan's Sharpshooters silence the rebel artillery:

Our guns keep up a constant shelling both day and night, which is seldom responded to by the rebels, because of the terrible Berdan sharp shooters who cover their guns to such an extent that they cannot work them. I never before saw such a set of men as these same Berdan sharp shooters. They are armed with the telescope sighted rifle peculiar to their calling, some of which weigh the extraordinary heft of 57 to 60 pounds. These men speak confidently of killing, without the slightest difficulty, at a mile distant. The impression left upon the minds of the soldiers by these people is not at all a pleasant one, and as they come out each morning after breakfast strutting along, the men look in askance and rather shrink from them. As far as I am able to judge, although receiving a general order to occupy certain portions of the line, it is left discretionary with them to select their own position. So that good service is done, the method is with the individual. It has frequently occurred that one or more of them have occupied my part and I have watched their proceedings very closely. They remind one of the spider who, hour after hour, so patiently waits for the unhappy fly. These men will, after cutting crotches and resting their rifles on them, coolly take a camp stool, and adjusting the telescopic sight, wait for some poor devil to show himself, when, quick as a flash, bang goes the rifle, and the soldier has solved the Trinity. I have often looked through their sight pieces, and have been amazed at their power and the distinctness with which objects of at least a mile distant are brought under the eye of the observer.

Richmond newspapers denounced the Yankee sharpshooters and advocated no quarter be shown to any captured sharpshooter. Eager to regain the initiative, the Confederate Congress passed legislation directing that each brigade raise a sharpshooter battalion and with the exception of the army in Northern Virginia, all Confederate armies complied. Since McClellan was threatening Richmond, there was no time to reorganize the army and even after McClellan was beaten back, the Confederates were too busy winning battles. Incessant fighting depleted their ranks and while some brigades or divisions wanted to comply, they lacked the manpower. A few brigades or divisions managed to raise their battalions but full compliance would wait for the spring of 1864 when Lee himself issued the order.

After Second Manassas (August 1862), Lee decided to carry the war to the North and hoped to capture Maryland. Unfortunately for Lee, his invasion plan was found in an abandoned Confederate camp and delivered to McClellan. McClellan marched to destroy Lee and after a holding action at South Mountain, McClellan found Lee waiting for him at Antietam. During Sumner's II Corps attack John Sedgwick's 2nd Division was flanked by that of Lafayette McLaw's. Fighting alongside the 15th Massachusetts was the 1st Andrew's Sharpshooters. They were doing quite well until McLaw's counterattack:

> The coolness and desperation with which the brigade fought could not be surpassed, and perhaps never was on this continent. Captain Saunders' company of sharpshooters, attached to the Fifteenth Massachusetts Volunteers, together with the left wing of that regiment, silenced one of the enemy's batteries, and kept it so, driving the cannoneers from it every time they attempted to load, and for ten minutes fought the enemy in large numbers at a range of from 15 to 20 yards, each party sheltering themselves behind fences, large rocks, and straw-stacks.

The Andrew Sharp Shooters suffered 26 casualties, including Captain Saunders and a lieutenant. They were overrun by the Confederates, and the survivors made their way back as best they could.

McClellan's failure to follow up and destroy Lee resulted in Lincoln's replacing McClellan with Ambrose Burnside. Burnside proposed stealing a march on Lee and marching down to Fredericksburg where he would cross the Rappahannock via pontoon bridge. Afterward his army would capture Richmond before Lee realized Burnside was gone. Burnside did steal a march but upon reaching the bank opposite of Fredericksburg, discovered that the pontoon train had not arrived from Washington. While Burnside waited, Lee rushed his army to Fredericksburg. Upon their arrival, they occupied Marye's Heights, just beyond town. An open field would have to be crossed by the Union soldiers to defeat Lee. Unsure of where Burnside would cross, Lee sent Jackson's I Corps south to block any Union attempt to cross at a lower point.

The pontoons finally arrived and the Union began building their bridge at night. Observing them along the waterfront was Barksdale's Mississippi Brigade. They wanted the Union to be halfway across and committed to finishing it before firing. Longstreet describes what followed:

> The Federals came down to the river's edge and began the construction of their bridges, when Barksdale opened fire with such effect that they were forced to retire. Again and again they made efforts to cross, but each time they were met and repulsed by the well-directed bullets of the Mississippians. This contest lasted until 1 o'clock when the Federals, with angry desperation, turned their whole available force of artillery on the little city, and sent down from the heights a perfect storm of shot and shell, crushing the houses with a cyclone of fiery metals. From our position on the heights we saw the batteries hurling an avalanche upon the town whose only offense was that it was near its edge in a snug retreat nestled three thousand Confederate hornets that were stinging the Army of Potomac into a frenzy. ... It was terrific, the pandemonium which that little squad of Confederates had provoked. The town caught fire in several places, shells crashed and burst, and solid shot rained like hail. But, in the midst of all this fury, the little brigade of Mississippians clung to their work ...

Undaunted by the bombardment, Barksdale offered Lee that "if he wants a bridge of dead Yankees, he can furnish him with one."

Four Union regiments conducted an amphibious assault across the Rappahannock. Intense street fighting ensued before Barksdale was ordered to abandon Fredericksburg. Burnside spent the remainder of the day crossing the Rappahannock and the next day in organizing the assault. It ended in failure. While sharpshooting did not win the battle for the Confederacy, it made victory possible. Barksdale's delaying action allowed Jackson to march up to protect Lee's right flank and stop Burnside's attack.

Following Fredericksburg, Joe Hooker assumed command of the Union army and divided his army. Leaving a smaller force at Fredericksburg, Hooker marched upriver and after crossing, swept down towards Lee's flank. Falling short of attacking Lee, Hooker halted at Chancellorsville. Learning that he had been flanked, Lee left a small force at Fredericksburg and marched north. Instead of attacking immediately upon meeting Hooker, Lee again divided his army; sending Jackson into the Wilderness to flank Hooker while Lee pinned him down. Mistaking Jackson's movement for a retreat, Hooker ignored the sightings. When Jackson's attack was sprung, it rolled up Hooker's line and only stopped because of nightfall.

Trying to stem the Confederate assault was General Amiel Whipple, 2nd Division, III Corps, who was singled out and shot: "Whipple was shot by a reb sharpshooter Monday morning. He was but a few rods from our Gen. and staff. I heard the ball pass close over me that struck him." Fighting concentrated between Hazel Grove and Fairview Knoll where the Confederate gunners on the latter pounded the Union line on the former. While the artillery dueled, Confederate battery commander Captain Greenlee Davidson was hit by a Federal sharpshooter. Lieutenant Camberlayne of the Richmond Howitzers reported: "I was on my horse beside Davidson when he was killed by a minie fired 800 yards off." The Union line broke and was forced to retreat under harassing fire of the Confederate sharpshooters:

> ... it soon became apparent that the enemy, far back in the woods—the margin of which our pickets firmly held—had gotten our range exactly, and from the tree tops at nearly a mile distant, their sharp shooters constantly picked off our men. Indeed the firing became so severe that we were obliged to keep below the breastworks for safety, and yet we could not see from whence the shots came. About 11 A.M., whilst momentarily standing in an exposed place talking to Lieutenant Thomas, he was struck in the shoulder by a bullet, which having traveled such a long distance was spent and did not penetrate

his clothing, but just gave him a severe blow and then fell at our feet. Upon examining the missile we found it to be of the peculiar elongated pattern used in the Berdan rifle and most likely was fired from one of those terrible globe sighted weapons captured from our people.

To stop the harassment by Confederate sharpshooters, the commander of Union III Corps, Dan Sickles, called upon Berdan's Sharpshooters:

[T]here were from each Co., by order of Gen. Sickles, selected from the 1st, to go beyond our picket lines, and ascertain, if possible, where the shots came from. But to proceed beyond the picket line, it required some caution and creeping, to get within sight of where the shot came from, but we became satisfied that it was a stray shot, fired from a target rifle at our pickets, who were on the rise of ground, and some of the shots came into camp. The party returned at dark, one at a time, one only being wounded, having exchanged several shots with the rebel sharp shooters, but not being able to reach the said target rifle, which kept up an occasional fire all day, wounding several men in camp.

The next morning, our regiment went out on picket in the vicinity of the target rifle. We started at three and advanced about one fourth a mile, and in addition to that, advanced four picked men in front of all others. Soon after daylight, there was a squad of rebs, fourteen in number, came creeping up to a clump of oaks, which they were permitted to gain without opposition, and then commenced an exchange of shots, which lasted for about two hours, resulting in one of the four on the extreme front pickets getting a ball through his leg, and others through their clothes, and the silencing of the reb sharp shooters, and recovering of fourteen rifles, one a Smith and Wesson rifle [actually a Wesson rifle], with a telescope sight, and the others sporting rifles....

Hooker retreated and command of the army now fell on Major General George Gordon Meade. With Vicksburg besieged, Confederate President Jefferson Davis asked Lee to detach a corps to relieve Vicksburg. Lee countered with a proposal to invade Pennsylvania to draw Grant away. Davis approved and Lee launched his second invasion of the North. Learning of Lee's movement, Meade rushed north where they collided at Gettysburg.

On the third day of battle, skirmishing resumed after the failure of Pickett's charge. Sergeant Austin Stearns, 13th Massachusetts, recalled how one comrade outwitted his Confederate counterpart:

[Charles W.] Comstock of [Company] K, during the days of fighting, was out on the skirmish line. The officer in charge of them cautioned him when he went out, telling him that there had been several men shot at the post he was going to. Comstock went out, keeping himself well covered behind the banks of earth. Firing was the amusement of both sides. Directly in Comstock's front was a reb who annoyed him much, for everytime he fired, Johnny Reb's head would peep up and he would fire at him. Comstock, finding out the trick of the Johnnie, though he would play one on him worth two of the one he was playing: so, taking a gun that had been left there by some one who had been wounded, he loaded it, and putting it over the bank along side of his own, pulled the trigger. Bang went the gun, Comstock having his eye along the barrel of his own, up came Johnnies head to take a look, when bang went the gun, and his head came up no more in sight.

Defeated, Lee retreated to Virginia and to Lincoln's chagrin, Meade failed to pursue and destroy Lee. Meade attempted to attack late in 1863 but the Confederate defenses at Mine Run were too strong and the attack was cancelled. In one skirmish, through a misunderstanding of tactical employment or a confusion of orders, a company of fifty sharpshooters armed with telescope rifles was ordered to charge the Confederates! Despite their clumsy and heavy rifles not being adapted for bayonets, they charged and drove away the Confederate pickets. Soon afterward both armies settled in their winter quarters.

In March 1864 Lincoln appointed Grant as General-in-Chief, in command of all Union armies. Grant came east to accompany Meade's army and in 1864, the two armies fought in the Wilderness, then Spotsylvania Court House, the North Anna, and Cold Harbor before settling down into a siege around

Petersburg. The siege lasted nine months until April when the Battle of Five Forks blew the Confederate flank open. An all-out assault the next day sent Lee's army reeling west. Richmond was evacuated and a few days later on April 9, Lee surrendered at Appomattox.

The Heartland

Only one Union sharpshooter regiment fought in the Midwest. Raised on the orders of Department Head Major General John Charles Fremont, no evidence has been found showing they fired a qualification score like their Army of the Potomac counterparts. Dubbed Birge's Western Sharpshooters, they were originally enlisted as the 14th Missouri Volunteer Infantry and were later changed to the 66th Illinois Volunteer Infantry. Two things distinguished them from line infantry and one was many of the men were equipped with sporting rifles supplied by Horace Dimick. The other distinction was that, per the *New York Times*, they wore "gray suits, and felt hats plumed with squirrel-tails dyed black …" As the war progressed many bought lever-action Henry rifles out of their own pockets and wore the normal blue frock coat and foraging caps.

Their division commander, Major General Lew Wallace, described them at Fort Donelson:

> A little before dawn Birge's sharp-shooters were astir. Theirs was a peculiar service. In action each was perfectly independent. They never maneuvered as a corps. When the time came they were asked, "Canteen full?" "Biscuits for all day?" Then their only order, "All right, hunt your holes, boys." Thereupon they dispersed, and, like Indians, sought cover to please themselves behind rocks and stumps, or in hollows. Sometimes they dug holes; sometimes they climbed trees. Once in a good location, they remained there all day. At night they would crawl out and report in camp.

Sharpshooters of 18th Corps

When the sharpshooters retired for the day, regular infantrymen kept up a continual fire during the night. This deprived the Confederates of sleep and wore on their nerves. In the morning the sharpshooters returned to continue the firing.

As mentioned, trees were dangerous posts since the sharpshooter perched in the tree once exposed was subjected to counterfire with no chance of safely descending quickly. "A sharpshooter, about three fourths of a mile off on the Federal side, had climbed midway a large tree and was picking off Porter's gunners. A six pounder was aimed at him and he fell to the ground dead."

After the battle of Chickamauga, the defeated Union Army retreated behind the Tennessee River at Chattanooga. The road that supplied it ran along the banks of the river and naturally the Confederates took interest in the road. While they were unable to capture it, they took positions on the overlooking Raccoon Mountain. From it they stopped the wagon trains by killing the mules. One Confederate describes it:

We had brought our Whitworth rifles from Virginia with us. These were placed down the River on our extreme left to shoot down the front teams, which after being done, the road was entirely blocked and we then proceeded in a leisurely manner to use our English rifles (Enfields). The road was too narrow between the bluff and the River for the teams to turn around or escape in any manner, and were compelled to stand until all were shot down. I saw one of the Whitworth rifles, an English globe sight carrying a large ball, a few of which ran the blockade, in the hands of one of our sharpshooters, kill two mules at one shot—the heavy missile passing through their necks.

The denial of the road meant that the supplies had to travel a longer mountainous route. Relief finally came when men were floated past the blockade and landed on the Confederate side. They drove away the Confederates and supplies could flow unimpeded into Chattanooga. Union reinforcements also arrived and defeated the Confederates who had been weakened after Longstreet's corps was detached to Eastern Tennessee.

Longstreet arrived at Knoxsville on November 17 and found the Union army strengthening the fortifications there. His sharpshooters occupied Bleak House, the Armstrong family mansion. From its tower on the third floor, and at 750–800 yards distance, Benjamin's artillery and lines could be seen. Standing in front of the battery was Union Brigadier General William Sanders who was mortally wounded by the sharpshooters. In retaliation a 20-pound Parrott shell tore into the tower killing one sharpshooter and wounding five others.

Longstreet's attack failed. Strung-out telegraph wire tripped the Confederates as they advanced. When they reached the fort's

Henry rifle.

ditch they found it was deeper than anticipated and worse, water had been poured down the embankment the day before and had frozen overnight, making it icy. Lacking fascines or ladders, it was difficult to climb and those who stood on the shoulders of their comrades were shot in the head as they appeared over the parapet. The defenders also rolled lit artillery shells into the ditch, killing many Confederates. Over 1,000 Confederates were captured and Longstreet retreated into Virginia.

After Longstreet marched north to Knoxville, the Union broke out of Chattanooga and forced the Army of Tennessee south past Dalton, Resaca, Dallas, and finally to Marietta where one Confederate, Virginius Hutchen, was ordered to the skirmish line. "My time has nearly come," announced Hutchen to his comrades. His position in the line was not enviable as there were several dead Confederates there. Turning over the bodies, he saw that each man had a hole in his forehead. Hutchen asked other soldiers where they had fallen and was directed to a tree that had a pile of stones alongside it. Crawling up to the rocks, he placed his hat on a stick and was rewarded with a bullet that pierced the crown. The bait had been taken. Hutchen repeated this trick three more times until he detected the smoke from the discharge. Hutchen then dispatched the Yankee sharpshooter.

Eventually the Confederates were pushed down to Atlanta. On the outskirts of Atlanta the soldiers of the 123rd New York Volunteer Infantry came under long-range fire:

At the top of this rise was the enemy picket line, where there were located several houses occupied by sharpshooters who could fire on us from the trees. We had a good view of the enemy's fortifications; where the road passed through their line they had a large redoubt with heavy guns. They could see our works through the openings in the woods and we furnished a good target. Their sharpshooters had long range English rifles that would carry about a mile and made it hot for us. The troops we relieved lost several men and the conditions were no better for our men. As soon as a man showed himself during daylight a bullet would come. … It was nerve wracking to know you could

Brigadier General William Sanders, killed by sharpshooters at Knoxville.

not stand erect without hearing a bullet hiss close to your head.

Under this condition the men were ordered to conduct a review before their corps commander, General Hooker:

We were ordered into the works at two o'clock for inspection. General Hooker, his staff and escort were to ride back of our works to view our fortifications and the troops of the 20th Corps. …Before he reached our position the General was notified of the danger and was requested to pass us in our rear, but having started to review us from the front he would not turn back. When they came to the place they were in sight of the sharpshooters, they started firing and continued to blaze away as long as the party was in sight. The General was in the lead but did not hasten the pace of his horse. … The General's orderly, riding almost at his side, was severely wounded, several of his escorts were wounded, and some horses were disabled. The General was very angry and as soon as he went to the rear gave orders to drive out the sharpshooters.

The 13th New Jersey charged at a double quick and drove back the rebel pickets. They then burned the two houses used by the sharpshooters and returned with thirty-three prisoners. Hooker was satisfied and rode away but "[t]he Johnnies were soon back in their rifle pits saucy as ever."

Eventually Atlanta was abandoned and, hoping to draw Sherman away from it, the Confederates marched north. Sherman occupied Atlanta instead and razed it. Ignoring the Confederates (who would be defeated at Nashville), Sherman cut himself off from his lines of communication and struck out for Savannah. His army would not stop until they marched through the Carolinas and into Washington, D.C.

Mississippi

Sharpshooting played a neglected role in the area around the Mississippi River. Confederate General Richard Taylor observed:

> It is curious to recall the ideas prevailing in the first years of the war about gunboats. To the wide-spread terror inspired by them may be ascribed to the loss of Fort Donelson and New Orleans. … It was popularly believed that the destructive power of these monsters were not to be resisted. Time proved that the lighter class of boats, called "tinclads," were helpless against field guns, while the heavy iron-clads could be driven off by riflemen protected by the timber and levels along the streams. To fire ten-inch guns at skirmishers, widely dispersed and under cover, was very like snipe-shooting with twelve-pounders; and in narrow waters gunboats required troops on shore for their protection.

Such was the case when smaller Confederate gunboats, *Josiah H. Bell* and *Uncle Ben* closed within rifle range of larger Union boats, *Morning Light* and *Velocity*, and captured them.

During one of the Vicksburg campaigns, while Admiral Porter's squadron was steaming up Steele's Bayou, it was caught at close quarters by the Confederates and almost everyone was driven below to the safety of the casemate. Describing their accuracy is Admiral Porter:

> I made the signal to retreat. … But just as I gave the order, half a dozen rifle bullets came on board, and one of them struck the first lieutenant, Mr. Wells, in the head while I was talking to him and giving him an order. He fell, apparently dead, at my feet. I called an officer to remove him, and he fell dead, as I supposed, on the other's body. Then an old quartermaster came, dragging a large quarter-inch iron plate along the deck, and stuck it up against a hog post. "There, sir" he said, "stand behind that; they've fired at you long enough," and I was wise enough to take that old fellow's advice. Poor old man! He was shot in the head as he turned to get behind his cotton bale.

The Confederates trapped Porter in narrow waters with a sunken coal barge and fallen trees. Whenever a gunport was opened, rifle fire poured in. Only Sherman's timely arrival prevented Porter from scuttling his squadron. Porter's memoirs are silent about it but Sherman's wasn't:

> I inquired of Admiral Porter what he wanted to do, and he said he wanted to get out of that scrape as quickly as possible. ... He informed me at one time things looked so critical that he had made up his mind to blow up the gunboats, and to escape with his men through the swamp to the Mississippi River. There being no longer any sharp-shooters to bother the sailors, they made good progress.

Had Porter scuttled his squadron, Grant may never have captured Vicksburg and would have been shelved as another failed general.

Grant finally hit upon a plan to capture Vicksburg. Porter landed Grant's army on the opposite bank of the Mississippi. From there they marched below Vicksburg where they again met with Porter whose squadron ran the gauntlet of fire as they passed Vicksburg. Porter then transported Grant's men back to the eastern shore of the Mississippi at Bruinsburg. After driving off the defending Confederates at Bruinsburg, Grant's army marched on Port Gibson where they defeated the Confederates posted to block them. They next marched on Jackson and drove any relief force back before swinging back west and defeating another Confederate force at Champion's Hill and finally, at the Big Black River. In two weeks Grant's army fought five battles before trapping the Confederates at Vicksburg. His coup de main failed to capture the city on May 19 and after an artillery bombardment to destroy the cotton bale breastworks that sheltered the Confederate infantry, Grant attacked again on May 21. That too failed and Grant settled down for a siege.

Confederate Captain Bell describes his briefing at the Louisiana Redan:

he carried me to the right side of the fort and, pointing to a solitary pine tree on a knoll probably five hundred yards away and with some forty feet to the first limb, informed me that every morning a Yankee sharpshooter would climb up in the forks of the tree, that he had killed one of his men and wounded several in the fort, that he had tried to dislodge him, but had not. Wishing me a pleasant(?) time, he marched his men out, and I took command. Next morning our adjutant, John Dupuy, and I were making an inspection of the fort, when our friend in the tree promptly gave us to understand that he was ready for business by sending several bullets near our heads. I called several of my best shots over and had them try their hands on him, but all failed to hit him, he made it dangerous for a man to cross the fort for several days. Finally a little fellow named White came up and proposed to go out at night, crawl close up to the tree before day, hide under the treetops that had been felled to impede the Yankees in charging, and, as soon as it was light enough to shoot, pick off the Yankee in the tree. I told him that it was a desperate risk, as he would be several hundred yards inside the Yankee lines, but he only laughed and said he was a desperate man. I consented, and he left the fort about 3 a.m. At daylight, with a number of our men, I was watching the tree and had about concluded White had failed, when I saw a puff of smoke rise from the brush about fifty yards from the tree. The report of the rifle had not reached me when I saw the body of a man tumble like a squirrel out of the fork some fifty feet from the ground. All was quiet for some ten minutes, when we saw a squad of Yankees move toward the tree. They found their man dead all right, but seemed to be puzzled as to who killed him. We opened fire on them and they picked him up and left. When White returned to the fort that night, he reported that the man had climbed the tree before daylight, but it was too dark for him to see the sights on his gun, so he had to wait. After shooting he ran some distance and hid in a ravine, where he remained concealed in the brush all day. He saw the Yankees looking for him, and several times they were close to his hiding place.

While conditions improved, danger was always present. "One morning Gen. Green, with two of his staff, came into our fort to inspect the position of the enemy in our front." When it became evident that General Green was going to expose himself, Captain Bell warned him off. "I warned him not to look through the portholes until we fired a few shots to keep the Yankees down." Green brushed off Captain Bell's advice and replied, "A bullet has not been moulded that will kill me." Bell described the predictable result. "He failed to heed the warning, and at the second porthole through which he looked was shot and instantly killed. He was a gallant soldier and a gentleman." Green's loss was felt after his brigade was paroled and many never returned. Captain Bell continues his narrative:

On the afternoon of July 3, about four o'clock, an orderly handed me a paper containing the information that Vicksburg would be surrendered the next morning, July 4, at ten o'clock. I gave Dupuy the order to read to the men, and I watched the effect. Some seemed relieved, some shed tears, and others swore. After the order was read, young White, who had shot the Yankee out of the tree, came to me and said: "Well, Captain, the time has come when I must tell you who I am." He then informed me that he had first enlisted in Gen. Grant's regiment in Missouri, but afterwards concluded that he was on the wrong side, he had deserted and joined our battalion. Grant's old regiment happened at that time to be in front of us, and if he surrendered death would be certain. He had heard of the man who had brought up the gun caps, and he proposed, if I would give him a paper showing that he had not deserted from us, to leave the city the same way. I gave him the paper, and that night some of the boys helped him build his raft and sent him adrift. I never expected to see him again, for the river was filled below with Yankee boats of every description, but one of the first men to report at parole camp in Hempstead County, Ark., was little Tom White. We surrendered next day and were kindly treated by the Yankees.

The only Tom White found in Grant's 21st Illinois Infantry was mustered in on February 4, 1864 and mustered out on December 16, 1865. It is likely that the person involved was George W. White of Co. D who "deserted to the enemy" on October 8, 1861. Postwar many former Confederates feared retaliation and it was not unknown for individuals to change their name to protect their identity.

Vicksburg fell on July 4, 1863 and Port Hudson remained the only obstruction on the Mississippi. Nathaniel Banks had been besieging it and it became a site for intense sharpshooting. Captain John W. De Forest, 12th Connecticut, wrote:

> From a distance of nearly half a mile the Rebel sharpshooters drew a bead on us with a precision which deserved the highest commendation of their officers, but which made us curse the day they were born. One incident proves, I think, that they were able to hit an object farther off than they could distinguish its nature. A rubber blanket, hung over the stump of a sapling five feet high, which stood in the centre of our bivouac, was pierced by a bullet from this quarter. A minute later a second bullet passed directly over the object and lodged in the tree behind it. ... Evidently the invisible marksman, eight hundred yards away, had mistaken it for a Yankee. Several men were hit upon this same hillock, or immediately in rear of it; and I for one never crossed it without wondering whether I should get safely to the other side... We lost eight or ten men during that first day, partly from not knowing these dangerous localities, and partly from excess of zeal. Our fellows attempted to advance the position, leaped the knoll without orders, and took to the trees on the outer slope, and were only driven back after sharp fighting.

Captain De Forest continued his narrative:

> On duty days we popped away at the enemy, or worked at strengthening our natural rampart. We laid a line of logs along the crest of the knoll, cut notches in them, and then put on another tier of logs, thus providing ourselves with portholes. With the patience of cats watching for mice, the men would peer for hours through the portholes, waiting a chance to shoot a Rebel; and the faintest show of the crown of a hat above the fortification, undistinguishable to that inexperienced eye, would draw a bullet. By dint of continual practice many of our fellows became admirable marksmen. During one of the truces the Confederates called to us, "Aha, you have got some sharpshooters over there!" After the surrender an officer of the Second Alabama told me that most of their casualties were cases of

shots between the brim of the hat and the top of the head; and that having once held up a hoe handle to test our marksmanship, it was struck by no less than three bullets in as many minutes…

The garrison gave us full as good as we sent. Several of our men were shot in the face through the portholes as they were taking aim. One of these unfortunates, I remember, drew his rifle back, set the butt on the ground, leaned the muzzle against the parapet, turned around, and fell lifeless. He had fired at the moment he was hit, and two or three eye-witnesses asserted that his bullet shivered the edge of the opposite porthole, so that in all probability he and his antagonist died together. It must be remembered that these openings were but just large enough to protrude the barrel of a musket and take sight along it.

Port Hudson surrendered on July 9 and opened the Mississippi for the Union. The strangling of the Confederacy was realizing fruition.

Battery Wagner

In the wake of the victories at Gettysburg and Vicksburg, Union Major General Quincy Gillmore wanted to add Charleston to the growing laurels of victory and take his place alongside Meade and Grant as a national hero. Since David Hunter's June 1862 attempt to capture Charleston and Du Pont's monitor attack had failed, no progress had been made against the hotbed of secession. Enter the conqueror of Fort Pulaski, Quincy Gillmore, who proposed a plan to capture it. Summoned to Washington, Gillmore outlined his four-part plan to capture Charleston. Gillmore pointed out that guarding Charleston Bay was Fort Sumter and if Fort Sumter fell, then Charleston would follow. First he would land men at the southern end of Morris Island. Second he would capture Battery Wagner and Battery Gregg, which guarded Fort Sumter's vulnerable southern wall. Third, he would capture Sumter itself and last, have the navy sail in and bombard or cower Charleston into submission. His plan was approved and Gillmore relieved David Hunter.

Gillmore's men landed on July 10 and easily drove the Confederates away from their rifle pits. Wagner's garrison was too small to counterattack but reinforcements were rushed to bolster it. They came in handy the next day when Gillmore attempted to capture Wagner by coup de main.

A more carefully planned assault was needed and Gillmore began emplacing artillery that could shell the fort. His attack was launched on July 18 and was led by the 54th Massachusetts. It failed with heavy casualties and Gillmore resorted to a siege. Observing that Gillmore forsook blood for shovels and sweat, the Confederates brought English-made scoped Whitworth rifles to the island. Lieutenant W. D. Woodbery led a detail of twenty-one men who trained on nearby Sullivan Island. Their presence was noted almost immediately when Union sappers were struck at 1,300 yards distance. With Woodbery's Whitworth-armed sharpshooters present, only light work could be performed somewhat safely during the day and any heavy work would have to wait for night. Long summer days meant progress slowed considerably.

Because the Whitworth fired a smaller diameter projectile than the standard .578 minié ball, its superior ballistic coefficient gave it greater range and penetrative power. The 6-inch-thick rope mantlets that had once protected the Union artillerymen were easily pierced by the Whitworth. This necessitated Gillmore's engineers to fashion boiler plates around the embrasures.

Since Union pickets were unequal to the task of neutralizing Woodbery's sharpshooters, better marksmen were needed than the pickets who had been relied upon to sharpshoot. Tests were held and the top fifty marksmen identified. They were detailed to an ad hoc sharpshooter company led by Captain Richard Ela and Lieutenant Albert Clay Jewett, 3rd New Hampshire. To select the gun for the ad hoc company, various rifles that were available on the island were tested and the most accurate one was the humble Springfield rifle musket. Placed in a separate camp, the men trained and when ready, took to the trenches with Captain Ela leading half one day and Lieutenant Jewett the other half the next. Each man carried 100 rounds of ammunition and his rations when he positioned himself in the advanced trenches. At day's end when they returned to camp, both rations and ammunition were exhausted.

While the Springfield is accurate out to 500 yards, the Whitworth far exceeded it, so the Union sharpshooters were disadvantaged until the distance was closed. To accommodate their sharpshooters, Union sappers left 2-inch loopholes between sandbags "at the proper distances" as they built the siege works. Like the Confederates, the men learned to darken the holes so as to keep their opponents from guessing whether a loophole was being used or not. Stepping up to a lighted loophole told the other side to fire a shot.

As the Union sappers worked their way forward, Woodbery's men were relieved by another ad hoc sharpshooter detail led by Lieutenant John E. Dugger, 8th North Carolina. Like Ela's men, for the duration of the siege, Woodbery and Dugger would rotate their sharpshooters on Morris Island, resting somewhere for a few days before returning to duty.

Even with the Union sharpshooters, the Confederate threat was not neutralized and one Union captain had all the fingers of his right hand cut off while installing a gabion. Another Whitworth sharpshooter twice shot the telegraph line that connected the front trench with Gillmore's headquarters. The Union suffered losses daily because of sharpshooting and to suppress the sharpshooters, Gillmore had his artillery bombard Wagner. Barrages became so heavy that most Confederates remained sheltered in the bombproof [shelter] and the only men who didn't were the Whitworth sharpshooters.

Confederate sharpshooting became so intense that a frustrated Gillmore pleaded with the blockading squadron's Admiral Dahlgren to have his monitors' guns bear on Battery Wagner to suppress them. When they tried, a saucy Confederate even shot at the gunports of the Union monitors as they rotated their turrets to fire. Gillmore finally resorted to a massive bombardment under which his engineers could work.

One particular Confederate sharpshooter earned the enmity of his Union counterparts and both Union Brigadier General George H. Gordon and Lieutenant Albert Clay Jewett mentioned him in their memoirs. Jewett wrote:

> while connected with the sharpshooters, I had many and various experiences and among them will mention a few. Not the least in interest were the exploits of one of the Confederates, a remarkable marksman, located somewhere about Fort Wagner. For some reason this man went by the name of the "n*****" sharpshooter. It may be he was one, but I always suspected that he might be a dark skinned southerner or perhaps a mulatto. This man was more to be dreaded than almost everything else opposed to us, for his aim seemed as unerring as fate, anywhere within the range of his rifle. His arm must have been some kind of heavy sporting rifle, as it was of quite large caliber and of astonishing range. He could hit the arms of cannoneers a half a mile or more distant if they exposed them in loading their pieces, and if any poor soldier revealed himself at any exposed point, certain death was his portion if the "n*****" was on duty.

The Confederates were not immune from sharpshooting and one Confederate picket received a ball down his barrel—the Yankee who fired it was that good! Despite their best efforts, Ela's men were incapable of silencing the Confederates. Another solution was tried and Gillmore brought in the extremely accurate Parrot guns that shelled and destroyed many of the sandbags behind which the Confederate sharpshooters had shielded themselves. The destruction of the sandbags was highly demoralizing too. As the Union lines approached closer, double barrel shotguns were retrieved from the Charleston Armory and issued to the sharpshooters. One was used once to kill one Yankee who got too close.

After fifty-five days, the sappers reached Wagner's moat. Gillmore's men were now positioned to storm Wagner in one rush and the date was set for September 7. When the first Union soldiers scaled Wagner's walls, they expected to be slaughtered like their brethren had been on July 18. Instead of carnage, they found Wagner had been abandoned only moments before. While evacuating Wagner, the Confederates had attempted to blow it up but the fuse failed. The Union soldiers rushed to Battery Gregg, which they also found abandoned.

They arrived in time to see the last boatload of Confederates attempting to evacuate the island. Firing upon it, they convinced the Confederates to roll back to shore and to surrender. Among them were several blacks and it required a lot of effort by the officers to prevent their men from killing them. While elated, Gillmore still needed to capture Fort Sumter before the navy could sail in to bombard the city. Sumter held on and Dahlgren, citing the torpedoes (mines) that could be activated from Sumter, refused to sail past the fort to bombard Charleston. Dahlgren had already lost the semi-ironclad *Keokuk* to a mine and declined exposing his remaining vessels to harm. Defending Wagner gave the Confederates time to improve Charleston's defenses. Gillmore for his part became fixated on his plan, wasted time and resources in a lengthy siege and was ultimately stalemated. Sumter and Charleston would not fall until 1865. Between Sherman's army marching up from Georgia, and Gillmore landing north of Charleston at Bull's Bay to attack it from the land, the Confederates abandoned Sumter and Charleston to the Union.

CHAPTER 5

FROM SHARPSHOOTING TO SNIPING

1866–1918

"He killed him right where he used to sit down."

Technological Changes

DESPITE SHARPSHOOTING'S DEMONSTRATED USEFULNESS, no lessons were drawn from it as the American army resumed its former role of a frontier police force. Experience of warfare against Plains Indians mounted on swift ponies led many to believe that sharpshooting was unsuitable for the army's challenges. Apart from in regimental histories or memoirs, sharpshooting was forgotten as the nation rebuilt and resumed the westward expansion interrupted by the war.

Metallic cartridges had been invented prior to the Civil War and were used in both the lever-action Spencer and Henry repeating rifles. The 1866 Austro-Prussian War was the last war where the minié rifle was used and both belligerents in the Franco-Prussian War of 1871 had bolt-action breechloaders. By the Boer War (1899–1902), black powder was replaced with nitro-cellulose-based propellants. Besides having a near-invisible smoke signature, smokeless powder also yielded higher pressures, a flatter trajectory and higher muzzle velocities.

The development of optical devices was not stagnant and stadia lines were introduced making it easier for the user to estimate the distance. Bubble levels appeared on both scopes and optical devices, alerting the user that the rifle was canted. These novelties vanished sometime after World War I but reemerged many decades later.

The American West

In August 1874, 10th Cavalry buffalo soldiers were with General Davidson who met in council at Fort Still with Kiowa sub-chief Red Food. Some Indians used the opportunity to attack the compound. Sergeant Shropshire recalled that he:

> noticed that a shot at regular intervals came from a neighboring cornfield. Under slight cover he crept up to the edge of rising ground, determined to locate the sharpshooter whose balls were coming closer with each discharge. Presently he discovered what looked like a shock of new cut corn. He watched that shock; he saw it move; there was an Indian inside it. The native had inclosed himself with green cornstalks; he was well disguised. Calling a corporal to him he pointed out the object and ordered a volley poured into the shock. The value of corning clothing fell in that vicinity. The next day the Indian's remains were examined and his body was found to have been pierced by five bullets.

One of the first American settlers in Arizona Territory was Pete Kitchen. A teamster for Zachary Taylor during the Mexican-American War, Kitchen joined the Gold Rush and afterward settled in Arizona's Santa Cruz Valley. At the outbreak of the Civil War, the Army went east and Kitchen was left to fend for himself. He was well prepared as his five-room adobe house had walls .65 meter thick and that extended 1.3 meters above the roof. Built for defense, the wall on the roof was loopholed all the way around. Dubbed Pete's Stronghold, it was the only safe haven for the hundred miles between Tucson and Magdalena.

Caliber refers to the bore's inner diameter. A .50 caliber bore is ½ an inch. A .60 caliber bore is ⁶/₁₀ of an inch and so on. The flintlock-era Brown Bess and Charleville Musket were .72 and .69 caliber respectively. The former was almost ¾ of an inch in diameter but most certainly loaded with a slightly undersized ball. Bigger and heavier balls were notorious for crushing bone; often necessitating amputation of the damaged limb. A smaller ball will render hors de combat and enjoys the advantage of yielding more balls per pound of lead—something that budget or resource-minded individual bore in mind. A pound of lead will yield approximately thirteen .75 caliber balls, fifteen .69 caliber balls, twenty .62 caliber balls or thirty-eight .50 caliber balls, etc. Modernly, caliber also refers not only to the bullet size but the cartridge itself; the 7.62 mm NATO was the standard .30 cal cartridge used by NATO forces during the Cold War.

Apache attacks were frequent and carrying guns was normal for Kitchen and his ranch hands. As a precaution, a lookout was always posted on the roof and through practice and with the aid of marking stakes placed around the house, the occupants knew the distance to adjust their sights. One day while digging a stake hole, Kitchen was attacked by a knife-wielding Apache. Unable to reach his gun, Kitchen bludgeoned the Apache with his shovel. Another time Kitchen spotted an Apache on a hill across from the house. The Apache jumped on a rock, turned around, bent over and showed his backside. It so happened that the rock the Apache was on happened to be Kitchen's regular target and Kitchen knew the exact hold. Grabbing up a rifle, Kitchen "killed him where he used to sit down."

Bozeman, Montana, organized an expedition of frontiersman into Sioux Territory. Sioux Shell Necklace harassed them from 1,380 yards distance. Resting a scope-sighted .44-90 Sharps rifle on cross-sticks, Jack Bean fired back and hit Shell Necklace. At Adobe Walls, Texas, buffalo hunters fled to the trading post before an Indian attack. On the third day, Billy Dixon observed a group of Indians lined up on the edge of a bluff. Using a scope-sighted .50 caliber Sharps, Dixon fired and knocked one down at 1,538 yards distance.

The Spanish–American War

Following the destruction of the battleship *Maine* in February 1898, America declared war on Spain and sent an expedition to seize Cuba. The Spaniards used smokeless 7 mm Mauser rifles to snipe at them and while the Americans had no sharpshooter units, they quickly improvised. Sergeant James W. Ford came under fire from one Spaniard:

> I was present with the attacking line of Troop B, Tenth Cavalry when it advanced on the Spanish fortified position of La Suasimas, Cuba, on June 24, 1898. I noticed Private William M. Bunn, Troop B, Tenth Cavalry, during the advance, whose conduct was conspicuous for coolness and gallantry, shown by the deliberate manner in which he kept firing at a Spaniard up in a tree, although the bullets were falling thick around us at that time. After one of Private Bunn's shot, I saw the Spaniard fall out of the tree and I feel sure that Private Bunn killed him.

Another 10th Cavalry trooper recalled searching for a Spaniard:

> They had been getting our officers in great shape, and we couldn't for the life of us locate the man or men who were doing it. Finally, bang! came a bullet which struck one of my comrades near me. I decided it was about time to look after that Spaniard; so I kept

a sharp lookout, and all at once saw part of a head peeping from behind a bunch of cocoanuts, drew a bead on it, and instant a Spaniard tumbled out of that tree.

Fighting alongside the 10th was Teddy Roosevelt's Rough Riders, who also came under sharpshooter fire. Roosevelt penned:

In our front their sharp-shooters crept up before dawn and either lay in the thick jungle or climbed into some trees with dense foliage. In these places it proved almost impossible to place them, as they kept cover very carefully, and their smokeless powder betrayed not the slightest sign of their whereabouts. They caused us a great deal of annoyance and some little loss, and though our own sharp-shooters were continually taking shots at the places where they were supposed to be, and though occasionally we would play a Gatling or a Colt [machine gun] all through the top of a suspicious tree, I but twice saw Spaniards brought down out of their perches from in front of our lines—on each occasion the fall of the Spaniard being hailed with loud cheers by our men.

To counter the Spanish sharpshooters, Roosevelt raised a detail to hunt them down:

I sent out that afternoon and next morning a detail of picked sharp-shooters to hunt them out, choosing, of course, first-class woodsmen and mountain men who were also very good shots. ... They started systematically to hunt them, and showed themselves much superior at the guerillas' own game, killing eleven, while not one of my men was scratched.

Eventually the Spaniards were pushed back into Santiago, as reported by Colonel P. M. Shockley:

In the trenches before Santiago, there was little firing at the Spaniards. The distance was accepted by most as being too great, and most of the regulars had not fired at distances greater than 600 yards. Of telescopic sights and mounts, there were none, and had they been available, the climatic conditions would have soon rendered them unserviceable. There were a few experts among the regulars. Inspector General Reader reported that: First Lieutenant Charles Muir, 2nd Infantry, is of the class of distinguished sharpshooters, known for ten years for his honorable identification with target practice. He is a man who mixes brains with gun powder and has the ability beyond that of neatly and correctly judging the effects of the wind, light and shade on a projectile, also the ability to have eye and finger muscles act simultaneously in pulling (the) trigger. While in the trenches … he saw a guard of the Spanish at a range of 1,100 yards, adjusted his sights … fired twice, called his shot instantly and each time brought down an enemy. Members of his squad, with equal success same time and range, potted a third Spaniard.

Lieutenant Henry D. Wise witnessed another amazing shot:

[D]uring the battle of July 1st, he and a sharpshooter named McIlhaney, had their attention attracted by a Spanish officer who was conspicuous because he was riding a white horse. Guessing the range, 1,100 yards, McIlhaney opened fire and hit the Spaniard. Wise says that he subsequently learned that Gen. Linares, the commander of the Santiago Spanish forces, rode a horse of that color when wounded, and believes that McIlhaney did it.

Defeated in both Cuba and at Manila Bay when Dewey's Squadron crushed the Spanish Squadron there, the war concluded in an American victory.

The Boer War

The allure of gold caused Great Britain to invade the Boer Republic in 1899. Anxious to defend their nation, the Boers organized into commandos and struck back. Unlike other opponents faced by Queen Victoria's armies, the Boers were marksmen and it probably didn't hurt that they practiced on 700-yard rifle ranges. The German General Staff noted:

Accustomed to exertion and to privation, the Boer possessed all the qualities which form the foundation necessary for success in war. When fighting against numerous, brave but badly armed native population, and when hunting game, he had learned to study a country, to avail himself of its cover, in order to get within effective range of his adversary, and only to fire when success was certain, but to fly quickly from danger. ... Nor did he lightly risk his life; he would quit a dangerous position without damage to his moral strength, and, instead of holding out to the last, he would occupy a new one.

Thus was strengthened the self-confidence of the individual rifleman who, in the field, remained always more a hunter than a soldier. The idea was that, in a fight, it was only necessary to defeat the adversary while securing his own safety, and that a hand-to-hand struggle at all costs was to be avoided. The tactics of a number of Boers was based solely upon the employment of individual and independent riflemen who, owing to the peculiarities of their race, were only unwilling subordinates, unless the objective were immediately plain to all eyes. Advancing at great intervals they endeavored to encircle the enemy, without exposing themselves. In the defense, which was favored by clear fields of fire and by the good cover afforded by the rolling ground and kopjes, the Boers had learned, in their struggle against the Zulus, what a terrible weapon is a rifle with sufficient ammunition in the hands of an experienced shot.

Their superiority in marksmanship was evident at Dundee in October 1899. To eject the Boers from Talana Hill that overlooked Dundee, the British assembled a force to storm it. Major General Sir W. Penn Symons dismounted and walked around to encourage his men. He was undeterred even after a staff officer was shot. He cheered his men on and stepped over a stone wall to examine the Boer positions. At that moment Symons was shot. The attack proceeded anyway and Boer Denny Reitz described the fight:

Our party under Issac Malherbe not one had been hit, but the Free State men had eight or nine dead, and fifteen or twenty wounded, the English casualties were about two hundred killed and as many injured, the disparity being due to the fact that the English soldiers were no match for us in rifle-shooting. Whatever the defects of the commando system may be (and they are many) the Boer superiority in marksmanship was as great now as it had been in 1881.

Among the British assault force was Captain Frederic M. Crum, 1/60: "It was a new kind of war. The invisible, galloping, crack-shot Boer, with the modern quick-firing long-range rifle, was thoroughly at home, and bravely defending his own home-land, with all its rocky Kopjes and Krantzes, its tricky spruits and dongas; while we, to make up for our slowness of movement, often had to make long and exhausting night marches over difficult ground." While attempting to flank the Boers, Crum was wounded, hospitalized, and captured when the hospital fell to the Boers.

Marching out from Ladysmith, the British came upon an abandoned Boer wagon. Some soldiers went to investigate and as the war correspondent Bennett Burleigh reported: "[t]he Boers gave them a warm reception, a number of their sharpshooters being concealed behind walls and rocks; and I, too, was glad to hobble back, for at 900 yards their shooting was passably good." At 1,200–1,600 yards distance the Gloucesters were relatively safe. However, when they advanced, they lost their colonel along with six others killed and forty wounded. Perhaps the most amazing shot fired during the siege was when a Boer proned himself and dropped a British soldier who was the middle man of three soldiers at 1,400 yards distance. Unable to break out of Ladysmith, the British resigned themselves to being besieged. Initially the Boers sniped at the British "from behind rocks a mile off" and when their confidence grew, they rashly attacked. The attack was beaten back. A relief column under General Sir Redvers Buller attempted to cross the Tugela River. Thinking the Boers had fled, he had bridged the river with pontoon boats. His 10th Brigade was allowed to cross unmolested but when the Somerset Light Infantry attempted to march in the open to cross, they were greeted with heavy rifle fire from 1,300 yards distance. They suffered 90 casualties that included four officers killed. Buller's relief column would have to fight several battles before relieving Ladysmith.

> The term **sniper** was coined by the British in 1773, but did not enter widespread use until the Boer War. Commander of the 10th Brigade, Major General Talbot Coke, used it in his report on their January 1900 attack on Spion Kop: "It is light now, and Boer 'sniping' commenced."

Four hundred miles from Ladysmith, the Boers were laying siege to Mafeking. Commanding at Mafeking was Sir Robert Baden-Powell, who bluffed the Boer observers by having his men simulate crossing nonexistent barbwire entanglements to give the impression that the city was well fortified. Dinner plates were used for a phony minefield in front of the trenches. Since wood loopholes were rendered ineffective by the smokeless cartridge, two ½in-thick steel plates fastened together at a 45-degree angle to form a 2 feet × 2 feet shield with a 2-inch-square hole in the middle of the joint. Finally, Baden-Powell applied a careful and systematic sharpshooting against the Boers that resulted in inflicting 40 casualties a month.

To defeat the Boers, the British resorted to removing their civilians into concentration camps and built a chain of block houses connected by barbwire to isolate the Boers. Starved into submission, the Boers succumbed to British rule.

World War I

Trench warfare and machine guns characterized World War I and stagnant positional warfare allowed sniping to flourish. This allowed for the periscope rifle, a modernization of the American Civil War concept, to flourish.

Australian Ion Idriess fought in Gallipoli as well as in the Middle East and this gave him an opportunity to use a periscope rifle, which he describes:

> The opposing trenches are so close that the loopholes are useless to either side. Any loophole opened in daylight means an instant stream of bullets. So Jacko [slang for Turk soldier] uses his periscope rifle and we reply with ours. A periscope is an invention of ingenious simplicity, painstakingly thought out by man so that he can shoot the otherwise invisible fellow while remaining safely invisible himself. Attached to the rifle-butt is a short framework in which two small looking-glasses are inserted, one glass at such a height that it is looking above the sandbags while your head, as you peer into the lower glass, is a foot below the sandbags. The top glass reflects to the lower glass a view of the enemy trenches out over the top of the parapet. It is a cunning idea, simple and deadly...

The German firm Leitz received an order for 10,000 periscope rifle rests from the Prussian War Ministry. These were detachable units that could be used with the ordinary service rifle. They had a separate stock that held the periscope and was clamped onto the rifle stock. The periscope stock also had a trigger that was attached to a cable that ran up and through the framework and hooked onto the rifle's trigger. Like its British and American counterparts, this invention allowed the soldier to safely aim and fire his rifle without exposing himself. Seeking to similarly equip its army but with domestically manufactured products, the Bavarian War Ministry ordered 2,500 rests from Bogen-Lampen und Apparate-Fabrik GmbH in Nuremburg. Initially mirrors were employed by Bogen-Lampen but as they tended to fog up, sealed periscopes were used in later models. Delivery was slow and by October 1917 only 432 had been received. U-boat periscopes were a higher priority for the firm. What ended the periscope rifle were unfavorable evaluations as well as troops' complaints about the weight and unwieldiness. No further orders were made.

Periscope rifle.

Captain Herbert McBride disliked the periscope rifle and complained, "The use of various skeleton mounts for rifles, by which the firer aims through a periscope and manipulates the rifle through a system of levers, never appealed to me. True, I sometimes used them, but never had much confidence as to my ability to hit anything …"

Other nations, including the French, Dutch, British and Americans, had their own variations. All shared in common the characteristic of being top heavy and awkward to use. The final German innovation was detachable radioactive glow-in-the-dark night sights that function like modern night sights. The rear sight unit had two horizontal bars between a V-notched peephole and the front sight a large luminous globe. Either unit could be attached or detached by turning a knob.

Germany

With the failure of Germany's Schlieffen Plan and France's Plan 17, the war on the Western Front degenerated into trench warfare.

Appreciating the lessons of the Boer War and in response to good marksmanship exhibited by some British and French soldiers, the German Army wanted scoped rifles. It was assisted by the General German Hunting Association President, the Duke of Ratibor, who in January 1915 appealed for scoped rifles:

> German hunters! You hunters in the homeland can and must help to defeat the enemy. The special conditions of trench warfare, which must be waged by our brave soldiers at short range on the western theatre, demand special weapons! A sure and quick effect against small, well covered individual targets must be heightened by particularly suitable weapons! These weapons, effective rifles with telescopic sights, are in your hands. On the request of the HIGH COMMAND and with consent of the WAR MINISTRY the FATHERLAND makes the following REQUEST: Increase your sacrifices! Give up your beloved weapons! Make your telescopic rifles available to our soldiers! Make the sacrifice that is not small for a true German hunter.

Over 20,000 hunting rifles were collected but after inspection many were unsuitable for the newer ethyl-alcohol-based propellant and spitzer bullet "S-Patrone" cartridge. The suitable rifles were marked with a "Z" on the butt and the unsuitable with a "M." The "M" stood for the older ethyl-acetate propellant and roundnose bullet cartridge. Even the rifles that accepted the S-Patrone cartridge were not ideal since their shorter barrels recoiled more and had a larger muzzle blast that betrayed the shooter's location. Until replacement rifles could be provided, they would have to do.

Starting in 1916 the hunting rifles were withdrawn from service and replaced with newly manufactured sniper rifles, the development of which began in 1914 under the Rifle Inspection Commission. With the exception of rifles made by Goerz, the Bavarian rifles generally had their scopes centerline with the bore whereas the Prussian-issued scopes were offset to the left to allow for loading via stripper clips. Bavarian scopes were 4×, had a vertical post and crosshair reticle and were adjustable from 200, 400 and 600 meters and the Prussian ones had a cross-hair reticle, 3× magnification with its wider field of view and adjustable in 100-meter increments from 100 to 1,000 meters. Each scope mounting system had its advantage and disadvantages. The rifles with offset scopes were difficult to aim through the small loophole of a shield. The centerline mounting system's disadvantage was that the rifle could not be reloaded rapidly, the sniper had to dismount his scope in order to reload. As the war endured, the distinction diminished and the Prussians adopted the Bavarians centerline-bore-mounting system and the Bavarians for their part the Prussian cross-hair reticle.

Initially each company was issued three scoped rifles (four in the Bavarian Army). By February 1918 the Prussian War Ministry raised it to five per company. It was generally left to the company commander to determine who received them. Unfortunately, the rifles were issued to the soldiers with little training nor were there guidelines to the company officers who distributed them. Some soldiers had superior field craft because of their hunting background. Additionally the Bavarians had greater familiarity with scoped rifles, cared for them better and used them more effectively than the Prussians who lacked hunting experience. Captain Herbert McBride shared some insights into the German snipers' skill:

> And right here I want to say that, at the short ranges—up to three hundred, possibly four hundred, yards—those German snipers could shoot. I do not think they were much good at long range; in fact I doubt whether they often attempted any of what we would call long-range shooting. I know we showed ourselves, with impunity, at anything beyond six or seven hundred yards. Sometimes they would snipe at us with a 77 mm wiz bang, especially if there were more than two or three in the party, but, with the rifle, never. The greatest range at which I ever knew a German sniper to fire at any individual was about five hundred yards. This fellow did get Charlie Wendt; but, as he fired some fifteen or twenty shots at me while I was administering first aid to Charlie and trying to get him under cover, and never hit me …

British Empire

The onset of static trench warfare was followed by German snipers asserting their dominance. Reported losses of "five killed per week per battalion" were initially greeted with disbelief and later frustration. Major Frederick Crum, now of the 8/60, described their plight:

> My first visit to the trenches left a lasting impression on me. ... We went all round the trenches, noting the hundred and one points requiring attention; but the thing which haunted me steadily after my visit was that the Bosche was undoubtedly "top dog" in the matter of rifle-shooting. ... At one point we crawled to an isolated trench, sniped at as we went, wherever the communication trench was exposed to view. Arrived there, we found the sniping particularly active. Bullets were ringing on an iron loophole plate our men had inserted in the parapet, and the tops of the sandbags were constantly being ripped open. The Colonel put his periscope up. It was shot at once, and he got a knock in the face. Covered with mud, he turned to his men and said: "We mustn't let them have it all their own way." But neither he nor I had any idea how the thing was to be stopped.

Initially the British gathered scoped rifles and, like the Germans, distributed them among the men who received neither instructions on sniping nor the care and use of scoped rifles. Major Hesketh-Prichard met one "sniper" who asserted being a dead shot at 600 yards. At Hesketh-Prichard's suggestion, he fired at a German loophole and his bullet was seen to strike six feet to the left of it. "I questioned the sniper as to how much he knew about his weapon. It is no exaggeration to say that his knowledge was limited." He added, "The men have no idea of concealment, and many of them are easy targets to the Hun sniper."

While the British officers were pondering their next move, the 4th Gordon Highlanders had Sergeant John Keith Forbes training its sniping section. As a child, Forbes carried a telescope during his long hikes in the Scottish hills. He became adept in its use and was a keen observer. Forbes earned his M.A. at Aberdeen

Major Hesketh-Prichard.

University and after becoming a teacher, enrolled into divinity school. War interrupted his studies and Forbes enlisted as a private with the 4th Gordon Highlanders. Sent to France in February 1915, his battalion served four months before being pulled back for a rest. During the rest Forbes was authorized to raise a sniper section of sixteen men. Drawing from the battalion's best shots and most active men, he trained them in marksmanship, use of the telescope, observation, recognizing and describing targets. Forbes also exercised them to develop their eye for the land and in camouflaging their posts. Range estimation and stalking over open ground in snake-like fashion were honed to perfection and when the battalion returned to the front, Forbes' men first neutralized and then dominated their German counterparts.

Being only a sergeant, Forbes' activity was limited to his immediate battalion. At the corps level, I Corps' Colonel Langford Lloyd began instructing snipers and he was soon joined by Hesketh-Prichard. Crum and some colleagues spent a day with 4th Gordon Highlanders' Sergeant Forbes and Crum wrote, "from that time onward I was sniping mad." In May 1916, Crum started his sniping school in the French town Acq. For field craft instructions, Crum drew from Sir Baden-Powell's *Boy Scouts Handbook* and in the course of operating the school, published a manual, *Scouting and Sniping in Trench Warfare*. After a month, his school was closed (19 June) and one month later General Skinner invited Crum to Arras to be on his staff as officer in charge of the brigade's snipers and Intelligence Section.

Not merely an instructor, Hesketh-Prichard was a practiced sniper:

> There were no loopholes in our parapet, and a little watching showed that there was a Bosche sniper quite close. He had a little door he opened and shut, and the plate above was a decoy, and the only way to get him was over the parapet. So I gave him a cap and a stick, and he had a go at that and missed it, I think. I may be wrong, but I think they expected me to shoot over the parapet, but this I refused to do. Instead of having a false loophole put in, I pierced our parapet low down just at his angle of fire. Some day when his little door opens he will get a bullet through it. Patience, I must preach, and again patience. I am determined that no risks shall be taken that are avoidable; it is the only way. Then I found a goodish loophole further down, and, therefore, put [a shot] through a German shield without getting any reply. This was quite a safe shot.

Patience paid off and the next day Hesketh-Prichard bagged his man:

> I killed that sniper at 11.25 today—very exciting. To continue from my last letter. They put in the loophole, and when I arrived the sniper Fritz had found it, and had blown it about. He had a telescopic sight,

Snipers of the 60th KRRC and 95th Rifle Brigade.

Frederic Maurice Crum (1872–1955) served in 1/60 mounted rifles during the Second Boer War. Shot in the right arm at Ladysmith, Crum was captured while hospitalized. Postwar, Crum transferred to the 2/60 and went to India. Before going to India he wrote his first book, *With the Mounted Infantry in South Africa.* Resigning his commission and going on half-pay in 1911, Crum worked full-time with the Boy Scouts. When World War I erupted he hastily reenlisted and in October 1915 joined the 8/60. Further to running a sniping school and writing a sniping manual, Crum continued providing sniping and scouting instruction and in 1917 he was responsible for coordinating the scouting and sniping training throughout the army. Post-war Crum remained active in the Boy Scouts and wrote two books, *Memoirs of a Rifleman Scout* and *With Riflemen, Scouts and Snipers, From 1914 to 1919.*

I am sure. He very nearly killed a sergeant who was looking through; another two inches would have done it. Well, it was impossible to shoot through the loophole, so I directed them to show a periscope near our loophole, while I went to the right, past the tree, and go up, and pressing my head against a sandbag, got a stick and shoved No.2 [plate] round till, with my head covered by No. 1 [plate], I got on to Fritz's plate. The first shot hit it, and I fired two more. Then as it was raining, and for other reasons, I went to smoke a cigarette in a dugout. While doing this the sergeant reported that the Bosches were mounting the shield with a white sandbag. This was splendid. Meantime Fritz had shot twice more at the loophole, so I went to the same place as before, and when Fritz, who thought I thought he was behind the plate, shot, I shot also. The shot went right into his loophole, and after it no more reflection could be seen, nor did he shoot again.

Sergeant Jack Winston, Canadian 19th Battalion, witnessed his lieutenant stalk and capture a German sniper:

Our lieutenant was looking hard across No Man's Land through the trench periscope, and I wondered what was keeping him so long looking at a spot I thought we all knew by heart. He stood there perfectly immovable for at least fifteen minutes, while several star-shells, fired both from our own lines and the German trenches, flared and died. Finally he turned to me and whispered, "Jack, I do not remember that dead horse out there yesterday. Take a look and tell me if you remember seeing it before." I looked at the spot indicated and sure enough there was a dead horse lying at the side of a shell-hole where I could have sworn there was nothing the day before.

I told the lieutenant I was sure that nothing had been there on the previous day and waited for further orders. German snipers had annoyed us considerably and as they took great pains in concealing their nests we had little success in stopping them. Several casualties had resulted from their activities. The lieutenant had evidently been thinking, while taking his long observation, for he said almost at once: "I believe that nag is a neat bit of camouflage. One of those Huns is probably hidden in that carcass to get a better shot at us." He then told me to have the men at the portholes fire at the carcass, at five seconds intervals, to keep "Fritz," if he were there, under cover—and taking advantage of the dark interval between the glare of the star-shells, he slipped "Over the top," having told me he was going to get the Hun.

Imagine my suspense for the next half hour. I kept looking through the periscope but for the fully fifteen minutes but could not find my officer. Finally I spotted him sprawled out, apparently dead, as a star-shell lit up the ground within the range of my periscope. As no shot had been fired, except from our own portholes, I knew he was not as dead as he seemed. And sure enough when next I could make him out he was several yards ahead, and to the left, of the spot where I had last seen him. Then I knew what he was after. He was making a detour to approach the carcass from the rear, and as he could only move in the dark intervals between star-shells his progress was, of necessity, slow. At the end of another fifteen minutes I located him in a position, as nearly as I could judge, about ten yards in the rear and just a step to the left of the carcass.

Sergeant Winston assembled a patrol to help the lieutenant:

[W]e ran straight into the lieutenant who was driving the Hun before him at the muzzle of his automatic. We wasted no time on the return journey but hustled "Fritzie" along at a brisk pace… When we were all safe in the trench, the lieutenant called off the barrage and the enemy in our front was doubtless wondering what it was all about, until the sniper who, as the lieutenant surmised, was hidden in the camouflaged carcass, returned no more. The Lieutenant had arrived at a point about five paces behind the Hun before the sniper discovered him, and then had him covered with his automatic. Like most of his breed there was a wide "yellow streak" in this baby-killer and he cried "Kamerad" instantly. By the time the Lieutenant had secured his prisoner's rifle our barrage was falling, and under its protection, he began his march back with the prisoner, and met us before he had gone twenty-five yards… The prisoner expected to be killed at once and begged piteously for his life, saying "he had a wife and three children." One of the men replied that if he had his way he would make it a "widow and three orphans." Needless to say he did not have his own way….

Another Canadian sniper matched wits with a Bavarian:

There was an old Bavarian sniper along this part of the front who had become famous for his killings. He had accounted for several officers in our brigade and the week before he came into this sector he killed a couple of our snipers of the 7th battalion. The post where they were killed had been given away by a new draft officer who did not understand what it meant to send his green men into a post of this kind, and having them banging and shooting at the landscape through it. I questioned this officer about it and he said the snipers did not use the post enough so he thought he was being efficient in sending men in there to shoot… The bullets that killed the two 7th Snipers came directly in through the loop hole[,] hit the timber and iron sheeting in the roof and glanced downward. This had been a good post and had been in use for a long time before the bright officer advertised it to the old Bavarian. This grizzled old Bavarian had been glimpsed on several occasions. He wore a beard appearing to be a man at least 50 years of age.

After the incident of the two 7th battalion snipers I quieted myself to the task of hunting for the old timer… I started out from our right flank into a maze of disused trenches that had changed hands several times and now were between the opening lines. They were filled with wire blockades or entanglements to prevent their use by either side in surprise attacks. … I worked my way forward cautiously till I thought I must be close to the enemy outpost positions. … When it was quite dark I caught a glimpse of a movement among that mess of wire. I did not make anything definite out of it that night. The following night I was back there again and set to watching that sag with its mess of wire coils. Dusk crept toward darkness and I was thinking about going in and calling it a day when there was a distant flare light. It lit up the skyline beyond that sag full of wire. There was the unmistakable outline of the head and shoulders of the old Bavarian. He had not taken the distant flares into account and he was outlined in a light that just enabled me to pick up the cross hair in the old Winchester A5 Scope. I fired before the light flickered and died out, then shifted my position off to one side[,] a bit of waiting for awhile to try to catch another glimpse of the spot by the aid of another distant flare. … I did get another glimpse across that sag full of wire. There was clear sky behind and I could not make out anything by the contour of the earth below. We never saw the old Bavarian sniper again, nor did I ever hear any more of him in the time we remained in the front.

To open the Dardanelles, the Australian and New Zealand Army Corps (ANZAC) landed at Gallipoli on April 25, 1915. Instead of advancing inland rapidly, they entrenched themselves in anticipation of a Turkish counterattack. The Turks also dug trenches and not having forgotten the lessons of centuries ago, began sniping at unwary ANZAC soldiers. As casualties mounted, reinforcements were needed and the Australian 5th Light Horse was called up and sent to Gallipoli where they fought as infantry.

Among the 5th Light Horse was Private William Edward Sing, better known as Billy. Being of both Chinese and English ancestry, he was ineligible for enlistment, as only men of European descent were qualified to enlist, but his origins were overlooked by the recruiting officer. Sing, after all, was an excellent horseman and the best shot in the Proserpine Rifle Club. Predictably Sing would be called upon to neutralize the Turkish snipers. Described as "a little chap, very dark, with jet-black moustache and a goatee beard," Sing's tally grew such that the Turks wanted him very badly. Ion Idriess recounted spotting for Sing:

> He has a splendid telescope and through it I peered across at a distant loophole, just in time to see a Turkish face framed behind the loophole. He disappeared. A few minutes later, and part of his face appeared. That vanished. Five minutes later he would cautiously gaze from a side angle through the loophole. I could see his moustache, his eyebrows, and part of his forehead. He disappeared. Then he showed all his face and disappeared. He didn't reappear again, though I kept turning the telescope back to his possy. At last, farther along the line, I spotted a man's face framed enquiringly in a loophole. He stayed there. Billy fired. The Turk vanished instantly, but with the telescope I could partly see the motions of men inside the trench picking him up. So it was one more man to Billy's tally.

As Sing's fame spread, the Turks sent their best sniper, nicknamed Abdullah the Terrible by the Australians, to kill Sing. Sing got him first and went on to have over 160 confirmed kills as well as another 150 probables. After Gallipoli was evacuated, Sing transferred to the 31st Infantry Battalion and was sent to France. Wounded several times, Sing earned the Belgian Croix de Guerre. Postwar, Sing returned to Proserpine and died in 1943. Sing is interred at Lutwyche Cemetery, Brisbane and honored by Australia with a bronze statue of a sniper behind a sandbagged loophole in Hood's Lagoon, Clermont.

An Ojibwa from Ontario, Canada, Francis Pegahmagabow was not formally trained as a sniper but his boyhood hunting and trapping experience was sufficient and he was near invisible as a sniper. Serving with Canada's 23rd Northern Pioneers—which later merged with other units to become the 1st Battalion, Western Ontario Regiment—Pegahmagabow was the most accomplished sniper of World War I with 378 kills and over 300 captured. While he aspired to pen his memoirs, Pegahmagabow never did and we have but one statement that attests to his skill: "The best shot I ever made, about nine hundred yards away, long distance sniping. Man on horseback. Yes I got him." He was one of only thirty-nine Canadian soldiers to receive the Military Medal with two bars.

United States

When the United States Army adopted the Warner & Swasey prismatic "Telescopic Musket Sight Model of 1908," it was the first army in the world to adopt a scope sight. Having a short eye relief of only 1½ inches, this 6× scope had a rubber eyepiece; later eyepieces had airholes punched into them to prevent suction against the eye socket when the shooter lowered the rifle. The scope base was soldered onto the rifle and added 2¼ pounds to the total weight of the gun. It was succeeded in 1913 by the Model 1913 which reduced the magnification to 5.2×. The locking nut was changed for the elevation knob and a clamping screw was added to the eyepiece adjustment knob. The Model 1913 was adopted by Canada and one mounted on a Ross rifle is displayed at Quebec's Museé Royal 22nd Regiment.

America's late entry into the war meant it could benefit from Canadian and British experience and the first American sniping manual was directly copied from Crum's manual. Besides the Warner & Swasey scope, equipment included the Winchester A-5 5× scope that was unique in having a tube bored from round stock. It had a simple crosshair reticle but others were available. It was unique in its time in having a groove milled on the underside of the tube. A spring-loaded plunger engaged the groove and prevented any rotation of the scope body while simultaneously allowing the scope body to move laterally. Not having internally adjustable reticle, the rear scope mount had micrometer dials for windage and elevation adjustment. Installation of the scope bases required drilling two holes in the receiver as well as two in the barrel. Criticisms against the Winchester A-5 included its high magnification with its small field of view, making target acquisition slow. The 6-inch space between the mounts meant the scope was not well supported and the scope had to be pushed forward of its firing position before the bolt could be operated. Afterward it had to be pulled back so it could be used. The narrowness of the ocular lens made it useless in poor light. Originally rejected in 1915, it was adopted in 1918 as an emergency measure. In Marine hands, the Winchesters A-5 scopes served as late as the campaign on Guadalcanal in World War II. It was also adopted in 1918 by the British and Canadians, who were desperate to catch up with the Germans and installed them on the Ross rifle and the Short Magazine Lee Enfield Mark III (abbreviated as SMLE Mark III).

Not all Americans were trained by British or Canadian instructors and Private Al Barker, 5th Marines, became a sniper without any training:

> I was selected as a sniper with a few others. … I climbed a tall tree near as possible to the German trenches and stationed myself there very comfortably. We could see the Germans setting machine guns in position to be used against our forces. We both had our rifles and plenty of ammunition, so we began to pick off the men who were operating the machine guns. … We succeeded in putting four of these guns out of commission when we were discovered by German snipers. I received a bullet wound in my knee and fell twenty feet to the ground. …

The most notable American sniper fought under Canadian colors. Eager to get into the fight, Herbert McBride resigned his captaincy in the Indiana National Guard and crossed the border where he was gazetted to the 38th Battalion as a captain. As the 38th was not yet mobilized, McBride was assigned to instruct musketry to the 21st Battalion. While there, he learned that the 38th was being sent to France first and resigned his commission to become a private in the Machine Gun Section.

M1903A3 Springfield rifle with Warner & Swasey optical sight.
(Springfield Armory National Historic Site)

M1903A3 Springfield periscope rifle in open and closed position.
(Springfield Armory National Historic Site)

McBride attended a sniping school near LaClytte and was issued a Ross rifle with a Warner & Swasey scope.

After sighting it in, McBride selected an observer who was not only a good companion but had keen eyesight:

> Early one morning Bou and I were stretched out in our little hole, he with the big telescope and I with my binoculars, scrutinizing the German line, about five hundred yards away. Suddenly the Kid says, "There he is, Mac, right in front of that big tree just to the right of No. 4 post, see him?" I shifted my glasses a little and,

sure enough; there was a man, evidently an officer, at the point he mentioned, standing upright, with a big tree behind him, and looking out over our lines through his glasses. Only the kid's keen eyesight discovered that fellow. I had passed him over several times, but, when my attention was called to it, I saw him quite plainly— through my glasses. When I tried to pick him up through the sight, however, I had considerable difficulty in locating him, but, finally, by noting certain prominent features of the surrounding background, I managed to find the right tree and got him centered in sight and cut loose. I got him.

On Christmas Eve an officer believed the Germans would not fire on stretcher parties and that it was safe to move in the open. As they crossed, an unseen German shot down one stretcher bearer, then another and finally the officer who was rendering aid to a stretcher bearer. McBride observed the shot and determined it came from a tree top in the woods behind the German line. Unsure which tree concealed the sniper, McBride opened with his machine gun. Other machine guns joined in as did an artillery battery. It is unclear who was responsible for dropping the German, but that he was killed was all that mattered.

* * *

By war's end, all major powers practiced sniping and the British sniping effort reduced British losses to "only forty-four in three months for sixty battalions; that means in three months … [a saving of] 3,500 lives." The Germans lost their initial advantage and Crum described the success of British sniping: "It was sometimes enough to kill a single really troublesome Hun sniper to secure complete moral superiority. In one sector, I remember, on our arrival, it was unsafe to show your little finger. When we came away, three weeks later, I saw one of our men coolly lathering his face in full view as he did his morning shave." Postwar, sniping was forgotten and overshadowed by emerging technology like aeroplanes, submarines and tanks.

CHAPTER 6

WORLD WAR II TO THE PRESENT

1940–

"Reach out reach out and touch someone"

(Telephone jingle adapted by snipers)

WORLD WAR II FOUND ALMOST ALL major powers unprepared for sniping. The Great Depression meant tight budgets for military development and when war erupted, the West believed that trench warfare would resume. The 1940 British sniping manual anticipated the use of decoys from trenches! The blitzkrieg on France proved its fallacy and motorized warfare effected a paradigm change. At war's outbreak the only major nation with any interest in sniping was the Soviet Union.

Soviet optics had their origins in the Versailles Treaty. Since the Treaty limited German weapons development, the Germans began cooperating with the Soviet Union to test new weapons and theory. Isolated because of their communist government, the Russians welcomed the Germans as partners and their closed society meant nothing would be leaked to the West. One of the pieces of equipment developed was the D-III scope which evolved in 1932 into the 4× PE, of which about 55,000 were produced before 1938.

By contrast the American military was not receptive to sniping and all scope development in the interwar period was done for the civilian market. Canada had only three hundred Warner & Swasey-equipped Ross rifles, and British scope development wasn't for rifles but for machine guns. Since the Germans were more interested in building the Luftwaffe, panzers and its navy than sniping, German optics makers catered to the civilian market to survive.

The Winter War

The Soviet Union asked Finland to relinquish land and when Finland refused, the Soviets declared war and invaded on November 30, 1939. Anticipating an easy victory, the Soviet Union invaded and the Finns held the Soviets at the Mannerheim Line.

Simo Häyhä was a farmer and when not farming, hunted and trapped. At age seventeen he volunteered for the Rautjärvi Civil Guard where Finnish Civil War veterans helped Häyhä with marksmanship. Häyhä was soon the best shot in his platoon and when he was conscripted into the Finnish Army for fifteen months, Häyhä was already a champion shot. On November 30, 1939, while Häyhä was attending an antitank course, a 450,000-strong Soviet army invaded. He reported to 6./JR 34 and fought in the battles around Suojärvi before being forced back to Kollaa. that Häyhä was an excellent shot, his lieutenant did not assign Häyhä to a squad but made him a sniper. His first mission was to locate and eliminate a Soviet sniper who had shot three platoon leaders and a non-commissioned officer. Häyhä waited all day motionless and as the evening approached, saw a glint of light reflect off the sniper's scope. Häyhä aimed, squeezed the trigger and killed the sniper. That was not the only time Häyhä was ordered to kill a Soviet sniper:

It happened once that my Co, Lt. Juutilainen, "the Horror of Morocco" as he was known from his previous service in the Foreign legion, tried to kill an enemy sniper with a scoped rifle. This Russian had taken up position about 400 meters from us and was constantly shooting toward our lines. After a while, the lieutenant sent for me and showed me approximately where he knew the enemy's sniper's position to be. One of our 2nd lieutenants was with us, acting as a spotter, when our duel begun. At first, I did not see a trace of him, just a small rock where he was supposed to be. After careful investigation, we spotted him behind a little hump of snow near that rock. I took a careful aim with my trusted M/28-30 and the very first shot hit the intended target.

As Häyhä's reputation grew so did the Soviets' awareness of him and they tried killing Häyhä with mortars or artillery fire. Injured once, Häyhä survived and joined in raiding parties:

By mid-December, the Russians had resumed their usual attacks, and after a while we started counter attacks on our behalf. The Russians were taken by surprise as they sat around four large campfires, and we crawled very close before opening fire. The resulting battle scattered the Russians in complete disarray and we captured plenty of booty from this trip. Among the items we captured were machine guns, submachine guns and four antitank guns.

Raids like this supplied the Finns with equipment that they lacked due to prewar budgetary constraints. Häyhä and another soldier once established an observation post within 150 meters of a bunker. From it they slew nineteen Russians. "After that the Russians built walls of snow to cover the bunkers and trenches connecting them."

Soviet supply troops were restricted to roads and the ski-mounted Finns often gained local superiority over isolated Russian groups. This forced the Russians to divert more resources to protecting their flanks. Ultimately the Soviets employed fifty divisions against Finland. Wounded on March 6, 1940, Häyhä never fought again but had amassed 542 confirmed kills and many probables.

Finnish sniper Sulo Kolkka is credited with over 400 kills. Like Häyhä he attacked the Russians behind the front lines in areas that they thought were secure. Kolkka also dueled a Soviet sniper who had killed most of the NCOs in one company. It lasted several days and Kolkka used his iron-sighted rifle to kill him at 600 meters when he rose to leave.

Defeated, Finland ceded 22,000 square miles of land. There was one final consequence of the Winter War: Hitler concluded that if Finland could bloody the Russian steamroller, then the Wehrmacht could destroy it.

Russia

Unlike the Great Powers, the Soviet Union prioritized sniping and opened several sniping schools. Men were selected from among the best of recruits and instructed in camouflage, sniping tactics, scouting and of course, plenty of shooting. Graduates were sent to individual companies where they paired up with another graduate to become the company's sniping team. To equip them, new rifles were needed and between 1932 and 1938, the Soviet Union produced 54,160 Mosin-Nagant Model 91/30 sniper rifles. High losses in the Winter War wreaked havoc on the Russian sniping establishment. Losses in equipment and the need to replace sniper rifles led to the simplification of the PE scope to the PEM; the latter differing only in that it lacked the former's adjustable eyepiece. By 1942 another further 53,195 telescope-equipped rifles were produced. Russian arms development was not stagnant and telescope-equipped versions of their semiautomatic M1938 (SVT) and M1940 Tokarev rifles were also made. Initially introduced for the semiautomatic Tokarev SVT-40 rifle, the 3.5× PU was later adapted for the Mosin-Nagant.

Russian snipers and sniping were not anticipated by the Germans. Panzer Generaloberst E. Raus noted that the Russians excelled at camouflage and wore "leaf suits of green cloth patches" as well as face masks. As to their effectiveness, Raus complained: "On 26 August 1941, while combing a woods for enemy forces, a battalion of the German 465 Infantry Regiment was attacked from all sides by Russian tree snipers, and lost seventy-five dead and another twenty-five missing."

Captured Russian sniper rifles were eagerly turned against their former users. Using a captured Mosin-Nagant sniper rifle, German sniper H. Jung racked up a number of kills. Still, it was insufficient and death due to careless exposure is recalled by another German:

> I returned from one of my visits outside to discover that Ludwig Kluge had taken my place in front of a black-out window. I didn't comment on it because Ludwig and I were close friends and had been together ever since we had first met while training at Herford.
>
> We were all feeling pretty good, and in the candlelight that flickered over the faces gathered inside, we began comparing our degustatory skills. All of a sudden a sniper's tracer bullet ripped through the window opening, striking the ceiling. Everybody jumped up looking for pliers or some other tool to pull the thing from where it had lodged in a wooden rafter before it caught fire. Ludwig remained seated the whole time so when I came back I asked him what was the matter?
>
> "I think that I am wounded," he said. I opened his shirt and sure enough, discovered the bullet had entered his back, angled down towards the ground, and ricocheted up to the ceiling. He had unwittingly exchanged places and the risks that went with it.

A priority target for the Russian sniper was the German sniper. A German explained:

> Our sharpshooters were killed because the Russians considered them primary targets. This was a result of the damage our sharpshooters could do, especially against the Russian commissars. With such

an emphasis placed on the sharpshooters, the Russians seemed to make sure that the sharpshooters were eliminated as quickly as possible. We had seen that thing happen and what it meant to us at that moment was that our sharpshooters were dying instantly.

One famous Russian sniper was Vassili Zaitsev. Hailing from the Ural Mountains, Zaitsev was taught hunting and field craft by his grandfather who was so skilled that he once killed a wolf with a mallet, thereby perfectly preserving the pelt. Drafted into the Soviet Pacific Fleet, Zaitsev was an accountant and payroll clerk before volunteering for the infantry and being sent to Stalingrad. At Stalingrad 1047th Rifle Regiment, 284 Rifle Division came under fire from a German machine gun that was 600 meters away. After glancing at them with a periscope, he took a snap shot and killed the machine gunner with one shot. When two other men attempted to man the gun, he killed them in quick succession. Unknown to Zaitsev, his shots were witnessed by Colonel Batyuk, who ordered that Zaitsev be given a sniper rifle.

As Zaitsev's fame grew, a political commissar ordered Zaitsev to start a sniping school. Having learned of a spring the Germans used for water, Zaitsev's small band pinned the Germans for four days. They shot up the jerrycans and denied them water until they were relieved. However, one of Zaitsev's comrades was shot, so Zaitsev went hunting for the enemy sniper. He noticed that among a pile of artillery shells, one shell had its bottom removed and was being used as a loophole. He ducked before the German fired and narrowly avoided being killed. The next day the shell was missing and Zaitsev used his periscope to scan. Finding it, Zaitsev had his spotter raise a helmet slowly. Falling for the bait, the German fired and, satisfied that he had slain a Russian, moved his head slightly. At that moment Zaitsev fired and evened the score.

Patience was also a necessary skill, and Zaitsev would sometimes wait for more important targets. One morning he and another sniper noticed a German soldier emerge from a thicket with a bucket in hand. He disappeared and then five minutes later, reappeared with two more soldiers who also bore buckets. Rather than firing, they let them collect water and return uphill. Later they spotted the German pouring water over the backs of three officers. While they were tempting targets, Zaitsev insisted on waiting. The officers were all company grade and he wanted bigger fish. The next day, Zaitsev decided not to allow the Germans to bathe. He deployed two other sniper teams within talking distance. A redheaded officer appeared from the pillbox. The snipers waited as the hat moved along the rim of a trench. Zaitsev figured there was an enemy sniper seeking to avenge the machine gunner they had killed the previous day. Even as midday passed, they waited. Then they noticed one single German appear with a bucket. He was unarmed; they permitted him to pass unmolested but stayed alert. Time passed and a thick heavyset colonel appeared. Following him was a soldier with a scoped rifle—their sniper! Next in line was a major who wore a Knight's Cross and then a colonel smoking a cigarette in a cigarette holder. This was the prize they had patiently waited for. Three two-shot volleys rang out and all four Germans died. The Germans retaliated with an artillery bombardment followed with an ineffective Luftwaffe strike.

Zaitsev once hunted a German sniper who had been preying upon the defenders of Stalingrad's Mamayez Hill. In anticipation of their duel, he set up three shooting positions. Afterward he left a helmet atop of one to see if the German would take the bait. It worked. Using a periscope, Zaitsev studied the terrain for hours before finally locating the sniper's post. He spotted at 600 yards distance an upright Maxim gun shield that was camouflaged with branches and dried grass. The aperture for the gun barrel was open and allowed the sniper to fire with some degree of safety. Sending a bullet through the hole might accomplish nothing so Zaitsev waited until he could see a helmet. Suddenly a helmet appeared but it was soon followed by another. Which one? A flash of light indicated a cup had been raised. If one German had delivered lunch, then the other was the sniper partaking of it. Zaitsev saw the cup raise again as the sniper threw his head back to empty its contents. At that moment Zaitsev fired and eliminated the sniper who had bothered Mamayez Hill.

The most famous duel involving Zaitsev was against a Major Konig or Thorvald from the Berlin sniper school. The story was originally told in Walter Craig's Enemy At the Gates and later fictionalized in the War of the Rats. Martin Pegler contacted Russian archivists who could not locate any accounts or record of the duel. Nor could any records be found on any Major Konig or Thorvald. Truth or fiction? You decide.

Twenty-five-year-old Lyudmila Pavlichenko was studying for her history thesis when Germany invaded the Soviet Union. Having taken up sport shooting at the Kiev Osoaviakhim, she was accepted into the army as a sniper. She received her baptism of fire at Odessa and when that city was evacuated, at Sevastopol:

I was often hit by shrapnel from shells that exploded some way off, but miraculously, I was spared any serious injuries. Sometimes, Fritzes would put on such "concerts" for a sniper! As soon as they found a sniper they would let fly. It would sometimes last three or four hours straight. So, there was only one thing I could do: stay down, shut up and not move. I learned a lot from German snipers, and occasionally they found me out. They would put me in their crosshairs, shoot and keep me on the ground, in a hole. Bullets would just whistle over me and hit all around; it was impossible to clear out of where I was. Then my gunners would give me cover and send a hail of bullets so that I would be able to get myself out of there.

The most important thing I learned from the Germans was how to set up dummies! Sometimes I would shoot and it would surveying an area and I would come across a Fritz and say to myself, "You're mine." I would shoot and it would be just a helmet set up on a piece of wood. Other times, they would make dummies so lifelike you thought they were real, to the point where I'd fire off several rounds, giving away my position and then the "concert" would begin. We always had a spotter who used binoculars and gave us the layout of the land, kept an eye out, and counted kills.

Lyudmila Pavlichenko with Eleanor Roosevelt in 1942.

To stay in the same spot for hours on end is extremely difficult and we couldn't move. There are some very critical moments, and you have to have incredible patience. For ambushes, we would take ration packs, water, sometimes lemonade and chocolate, even though chocolate was not part of sniper provisions. My first rifle was destroyed close to Odessa, the second defending Sevastopol. Actually I always had two rifles on me, one for show and another for work. I also had a nice pair of binoculars. The day generally started around four o'clock in the morning, if we had to get behind enemy lines. Occasionally, you stay in position all day and no opportunity presents itself. But if you stay like that for three days and aren't able to get at least one target in your sights, upon arriving back at camp you are so filled with anger, in such a bad mood, that no one dares talking to you. Luckily I was well-prepared physically and could hold out for many hours in an ambush. But sometimes, especially in the beginning you can't sit still, you give your position away, especially in the beginning, you say to yourself, "When your head is not in it, you need your legs." Lucky for me, gunners often came to my rescue.

Pavlichenko was credited with 309 kills when, in 1942, she joined a Russian delegation visiting Canada and the United States. During her tour, she gave talks encouraging the fight against Germany. After returning home, she was awarded the Hero of the Soviet Union and as a sniping instructor, passed her experiences onto new snipers.

Pavlichenko was only one of many Soviet women who fought as snipers, other notable female snipers included Nina Petrova with 122 kills, Nina Obkovskaya with 89, and Maria Ivushkina with 75. Altogether six women snipers were made Hero of the Soviet Union, all graduates of the Central Women's School of Sniper Training.

British sniper Captain Clifford Shore saw some Russians shoot and concluded that for a more accurate accounting, the Soviet claims should be divided by 100. Shore believed that Soviet snipers with a hunting background were skilled snipers but the propagandistic claims of 304 men killed with only 304 bullets fired were incredible.

Germany

During 1939 the Germans revisited the turret-mounting system originally used in World War I. A limited number of turret-mounted Zielferrohrkarabiner 98K were fitted with 4× Zeiss or Zielvier scopes. The scope bases were soft-soldered and screwed onto the receiver. These were high mounts that permitted the iron sights to be used. Also developed in 1939 was the ZF-41 1.5× long eye relief scope. A marksman scope, its low magnification and its small lens, which limited light-gathering ability, made it unsuitable for sniping but with the demand for optically equipped rifles, the ZF-41 was issued to snipers until better optics could be provided. Easily the worst optical device fielded by any army, ironically it was also the Wehrmacht's most issued scope.

Impetus for scoped rifles came from the soldiers. As the Wehrmacht invaded Norway, small bands of Norwegian soldiers used their limited number of diopter-sighted rifles to ambush Germans whenever and wherever the terrain favored it. The wily Norwegians would afterward escape to the next ambush position. Since the German soldiers' pleas (initially) fell on deaf ears, their own regimental gunsmiths began modifying the rifles for scopes. In response to the demand, surviving scoped rifles from the Reichswehr were retrieved from storage and pressed into service. Perhaps the most fielded sniping system was the claw-mount system: two steel blocks were soldered on the left side of the receiver. Each block had a cavity into which the claw of the scope ring fitted. A button in the rear base was pushed to secure the claw into place. Over 10,000 were produced during the war. New mounting systems were also being issued and in 1944 a side-mounted, detachable system was introduced. The various scope-mounting systems and optical devices used meant the German sniping rifles was anything but uniform. Besides the Mauser 98K, later in the war some semiautomatic Gew.-41, Gew-43 and the FG-42 were adopted for optical devices.

In 1942 the German army began formalizing sniping and attempted to standardize the equipment in use. Guidelines for snipers were issued and sniping instruction began in May 1943. Thirty schools were established, including institutions in Döberitz, Döllersheim, Hammelburg, Hohenfels, Müsingen, Wandern, Seetaleralpe, Oksbøl, and Kienschlag, with a capacity of training 200 soldiers per month. Training included distance estimation, observation and reporting, map reading, instruction on the sniper rifle and the scope, camouflage and field craft, use of dummies, night shooting only guided by sound, moving targets working in pairs, spotting, and marksmanship out to 800 meters. Depending on the stage of the war and the location of the school, German sniping schools varied in duration. H. Jung's training was ten days, W. Rohde's two weeks, Sepp Allerberger's twenty-seven days and Bruno Sutkus' the longest at five months.

H. Jung was seventeen when he completed training and found himself in the 7th Panzer Division in Russia. Attached to a pioneer unit, he volunteered for sniper school to escape from the front; even if it were only momentarily. Upon completion Jung and his comrade were transferred from their platoon to the regiment. From there they were given assignments and if there were none, allowed to operate independently. Jung didn't have

Views of Mauser 98K with ZF-41 scope. (Michael Tahirak)

to wait long before being called up to where a soldier was being killed everyday by a Russian sniper. They played a cat and mouse game for two days and Jung was taxed by it:

The following day was almost my last day on Earth. It began just like the day before, teasing and spotting for shots from the Russians. The hours were passing very slowly and there is no way for me to describe the tension that kept every nerve in my body as tight as wire. I was looking with my field glasses every chance I got. That meant peeking over the edge of the trench and then dropping back before the Russian could send a bullet after me. There was one spot I hadn't paid a great deal of attention to, a big broad-leaf tree. I took one more look at that tree and when I did, a bullet sapped in the air as it went within an inch of my ear, I felt the wind.

A close miss will usually scare the hell out of you. There were other times when I was missed by just a little bit and it would almost unnerve me. That's not what happened this time although I should have been very scared. This time I was simply mad, I felt almost raging but not to the point where I lost control. That close miss was one of the closest misses I can recall but there was more to it, now I knew where he was, I had seen him move.

The Russian sharpshooter was in that tree. Then I began to play a real guessing game with myself. The Russian had seen me too, that was obvious, and if I was going to try to shoot him I should move to a new position in the trench. I thought, "Wouldn't the Russian expect me to move, wouldn't he be looking for me somewhere else?" I decided, very quickly to shoot from where I was, without re-positioning myself. I would get only one chance and this was it.

Hans had watched all this time and when I started to get up so I could train my rifle over the trench he began to yell at me. He told me to get down, the Russian had me spotted. I heard those words but I was already in motion. I found the Russian in my scope. He saw a movement later but he had been looking for me at another point along the trench. I could watch him move, he was swinging his rifle around to aim at me. This picture in my mind is vivid and it seems like slow motion. The Russian was leaning his eye to his scope when I fired. Immediately after my shot, I fell back to the floor of that trench.

Hans was watching the Russian's position when I fired. He couldn't actually see the shooter from where he was but he did see the man fall. I had hit him. That was not my longest shot but it was the most difficult, about 500 meters.

Josef "Sepp" Allerberger, 3rd Gebirgsjäger Division, didn't like being a machine gunner. Machine guns always attracted the attention of enemy machine guns, mortars, and snipers. Injured by a splinter, Allerberger was granted two weeks' medical convalescence and sent to the regimental reserve where, under the supervision of the regimental armorer, he applied his carpentry skills to repairing stocks. While rummaging through some captured Russian weapons, he found a Mosin-Nagant sniper rifle. With permission, he borrowed it and after practice, was able to consistently hit matchboxes at 100 yards. The armorer was impressed and when Allerberger was released to full duty, gave Allerberger the rifle with the instruction, "Show Ivan what you can do!"

Welcomed back, his company commander had no objection to Allerberger serving as a sharpshooter, as he felt there were not enough of them to counter the Russian snipers. Familiarizing himself with the situation, Allerberger began inspecting the trenches and talking with the soldiers when he was pulled aside by the machine-gun platoon commander who complained about a hidden Russian sniper who shot everything in front of him.

Borrowing a pair of binoculars, Allerberger studied the terrain through a gap between the logs of the trench's parapet. Rolling up a blanket and putting a cap on it, he slowly raised it over the parapet. The Russian fired and Allerberger saw the faint smoke rise as well as a glint off the scope. Setting aside the blanket roll, he placed his gun between the logs to aim. He was unable to use his scope since the log obstructed the view, but as the Russian was only 90 yards away, it was an easy shot with iron sights. The eyes of the company were riveted on Allerberger. He fired and another soldier joyously yelled out that he had got him. Allerberger had his first confirmed kill.

During a retreat, Allerberger's regiment was attempting to withdraw when its reserve battalion suddenly came under sniper fire. Eleven *jägers* had already fallen and when two company commanders rose to get a better look, they were killed by headshots. Allerberger recalled:

> The number of hits led to only one conclusion: the battalion was facing a sniper company! We had heard rumors of such a thing, but so far had only ever come up against marksmen operating singly. Lacking artillery or mortars the battalion was helpless. Fire was coming from the impenetrable vegetation of a small forest of conifers. Bursts of MG-fire had no apparent effect and the devastating response it evoked was usually fatal for the machine gunner who tried it.

Pleas for artillery went unanswered and Allerberger was sent instead. After being briefed, Allerberger made five dummies which he distributed. He then pulled out his half umbrella frame and placed grass around it to match the terrain. The soldiers with the dummies were shown hand signals to raise the dummies on cue. Using this deception, Allerberger crawled out to where he could study the trees 300 yards away. He returned and conferred with the sergeant who was now commanding the two companies. They deployed their machine guns with a good field of fire and some protection:

To the side some distance away a rifleman waited to operate a lure. While I observed the woodland through binoculars, on my instructions he raised it from cover slowly. If it attracted a shot, I would identify the location from where it had originated. The MG would then fire a burst in the general direction of the trees, masking my aimed round. It was important to conceal from the Soviets the fact that they had a sniper working against them.

The tactical battle began. The lure rose and received three rounds as if to order. I saw the movement in the trees, took aim, waited for the machine gun to fire, then pulled the trigger. One by one the Russian snipers dropped from the trees, dead. After a quick change of position, a new round of the duel began. Within an hour I had reckoned on eighteen kills but still the lures drew fire. It was at about five in the afternoon, and an hour since the last shot had been loosed off from the woods, that the sergeant decided on storming the woods under the cover of the two mgs and myself. They reached the woods unopposed, looked with astonishment at the corpses and gesticulated wildly for us to join them. Cautiously, unhappy with the deceptive lull, we crossed the open land to the trees. ... It was the first time we had come up against female front-line warriors. As we stood over their dead bodies, some were shattered, bloody masks of flesh and bone instead of faces and features, we all felt a sense of revulsion and shame even though we knew that there had been no alternative.

Britain

When the British Expeditionary Force sailed for France in September 1939, it carried WWI-vintage scope-equipped P-14 No. 3(T) rifles drawn from storage. Most were lost during the Battle of France and evacuation of Dunkirk. A new rifle was needed and the SMLE Mk IV would have to do. As no optics were developed for sniping, the 3× No 32 scope developed for the BREN gun was adopted. Rifles capable of 2-inch Minute of Angle (MOA) at 100 yards were selected as a basis for the Enfield No 4(T). Modification began by attaching two pads that served as bases to the receiver. These were both pinned and screwed into the receiver. Each pad accepted a knob that screwed the scope mount to the bases. The actions were bedded to ensure a good fit and a wood cheekpiece added that raised the comb for a better cheek weld.

Training picked up in earnest and besides referring to the old manuals, instructors from Hesketh-Prichard's school were recalled to service. By 1944, the battalions that liberated Europe had a sniper section attached to the battalion headquarters. Corporal Arthur Hare, 15th Scottish Division, belonged to his battalion's seven-man sniper section. Hare and three other snipers were in a house between the lines where Hare was watching a German sentry 150 yards away. Hare also studied a boarded-up house 350 yards distant and while no smoke emanated from it, was certain it was occupied. Hours passed and using iron sights, Hare shot the sentry. Gunfire and artillery broke out, Hare had stirred a hornet's nest. He then remembered the house and attaching the scope, had just sighted it on the door when a shell hit its roof. A panicked German officer dashed out about 3 yards before Hare's bullet nailed him. Working the bolt Hare saw another German officer emerge and Hare's third bullet sent him leaping into the air. The third officer got 20 yards before Hare nailed him. Two more emerged and only the last one got away. Hare's sergeant called him downstairs and as Hare turned, he saw his battalion advancing. His first shot had coincided with an assault that Hare was unaware of. For this action, Hare received the Military Medal.

At Baussem, Hare was ordered to investigate activity north of their position. Hare took another sniper, Packham, and started early in the morning. They were moving into a room at first light when a bullet smashed the glass and ricocheted around the room. Flattening out, they realized they were under fire from a German sniper. Edging to the back of the room, they rose slowly when another bullet came through the window, narrowly missing them. That confirmed it. They were faced with a German who had optical sights. Placing a cushion on a rifle butt, Packham slowly raised it to the window while Hare watched. It had risen no more than 1 inch when the third bullet knocked it off. That was enough for Hare to spot a slight movement of a curtain. He summoned Packham over who carefully wiggled across the floor before sliding up into the shadow cast against the wall. Hare pointed out a corner house two streets away. The next time the curtain moved, both men fired. There was no more threat from that window.

Hare and Packham's encounter with a German sniper was not unique. Sergeant Harry Furness was summoned to remove a German sniper who had been inflicting casualties on a forward company:

[O]ver a long time no further shots were fired, I continue to search for signs using my more powerful scout telescope, and one house I watched for a while . . . had broken windows and damaged exterior wooden shutters . . . but now and again one of the shutters moved as the wind caught it. I must have been watching the area and that swaying shutter for hours when I caught a little movement—quick movements of any kind draw your eye to it if you are looking. I switched from my telescope to pick up my rifle and it seemed to me to be a hand reaching to get hold of one of the shutter by the edge. I fired immediately into and near the edge of the shutter, and even with the rifle recoil I felt sure I had seen an arm inside the house slide down and bang on the sill. I waited and watched until dusk before I left but saw no more movement nor had any shot been fired all the time I was there. That night a fighting patrol was sent out and they brought back for me a semi-automatic G43 rifle fitted with a telescopic sight. On the floor next to the window was a dead German.

United States

Like other Western powers, the United States was unprepared for sniping and its sniping equipment was obsolete. The Army adapted the M1903A3 Springfield rifle by installing a Redfield Junior Base and ring set. The low 2.5× Weaver 330 Scope with a crosshair reticle was adapted as the M73B1. The vertical picket post with two horizontal pickets on either end became the M73B2. Like the Winchester A-5, the M73B1 and M73B2's narrow tube meant it had a small ocular lens and poor performance under low light conditions. Since it wasn't hermetically sealed, it was susceptible to condensation and the lens had to be removed to drain it. The M73B1/2 bears the dubious distinction of being slightly better than Germany's ZF-41. The Marine Corps went a different route and installed the 8× Unertl scope on the Springfield. While it gave the marine snipers the ability to hit at 1,000 yards, the Unertl was fragile and required delicate care from its user.

Following the adoption of the U.S. Rifle Caliber .30 M1 (aka M1 or M1 Garand or even Garand), the Army realized that a sniper version would be useful. Numerous examples were submitted and the M1E7 from Griffin & Howe was adopted as the M-1C. Disliked by the Garand's inventor, John Garand, the unhardened receivers were sent to Griffin & Howe in New York where they were drilled with five holes, tapped in three of them and pinned in the remaining two for the scope base. The assembled receiver would then be returned as a unit to Springfield Armory for hardening. Since the receiver and the scope base were fabricated from two different steels, it wasn't unknown for one to warp during the hardening process—not the most conducive thing for accuracy. The M-1C mounted the 2.2× Lyman Alaskan scope as the M81 or M82. One of the few sealed scopes of the period, the former had crosshairs and the latter a tapered post reticle.

Garand preferred his own design, the M1E8, which was later adopted post-war as the M-1D. It consisted of a mounting block with a threaded hole that was slipped over the slightly turned down barrel and pinned in place. The final modification included shortening the handguard. The scope base and scope was afterward screwed into the mounting block. The M-1D with its 2.2× M-84 scope was quicker, easier and less expensive than the M-1C. The M-84 featured synthetic rubber gaskets for greater weather proofing and was meant to replace the M81/M82 as they became unserviceable. Only a handful of M-84s were made before the war ended.

Within the U.S. Army, a 1944 infantry battalion was allotted nine sniper 03A4 rifles (or one for each infantry platoon)—if they were available. No sniper training was provided to the men and officers were not instructed on sniper deployment. Distribution was haphazard and Sergeant William E. Jones, Company I, Eighth Infantry Regiment received his 03A4 sniper rifle because he was the best shot in the company. Private Charles Davis, Company L, Third Battalion, 415 Infantry Regiment received his M1903A4 because he asked for it. Private Robert Palassou of Company L, 363 Infantry Regiment turned in his M1903A4 when he transferred from one platoon to another. Private John Bistrica, Charlie Company, 16th Infantry, was given a sniper rifle by his lieutenant and told to climb a tree to snipe Germans. Fortunately his captain countermanded the order and probably saved him. Unlike most GIs, who carried the M1903A4 sniping rifle, Sergeant John Fulcher of the 36th Division received some sniper training in the states before being shipped out to Italy. This haphazard approach to sniping meant the United States Army did not field an effective sniper component during World War II. There were expert riflemen who gave a good account of

Sniper versions of the Garand and any other **semiauto rifle**—including the Tokarev, Simonovs as well as the German semiautomatics and sturmgewehrs of that era adapted for sniping—shared one common problem: they were inherently less accurate than their bolt-action counterparts. While the barrel is 90 percent of any rifle's accuracy, other factors come into play and the greater the number of moving parts in an action, the more difficult it becomes to ensure consistent movement among the parts. Called harmonics, any inconsistency meant that the gun could have a different point of impact with each shot. Bear in mind the trade-off a designer must make between reliability, which may demand looser tolerances, and accuracy. It does not take much pressure on a barrel to shift its point of impact (hence the use of heavier barrels on modern sniper rifles). Knowing this, attachments like flash hiders for the M-1C or M-1D were often discarded or removed in the field—their attachment not only shifted the point of impact, it opened up the group.

themselves, but the potential was never fully realized.

Despite this, some positive results were obtained. In Sicily an American column en route to Palermo was held up on the San Giuseppe Pass by a German 88 supported by an infantry platoon. The narrowness of the pass meant the tanks couldn't outflank the 88. Lieutenant J. K. Maupin from Missouri moved his platoon up a cliff on one side of the pass and after deploying the machine gun on the opposite side of the pass had his men open fire at 500 yards distance. His two snipers killed the machine-gun crew. The 88's crew was safely behind the gunshield and immune from bullets. Maupin left one squad behind to keep the 88 crew behind the shield and with the rest of the platoon, flanked the 88 and drove the crew off.

In Italy, Private James J. McGill, 34th Infantry, was patrolling with his squad when they bumped into a German patrol. McGill went prone and estimating the distance, adjusted his scope. His first two shots went low but his third dropped a German. McGill got two more and nicked a fourth when a machine gun at 600 yards distance fired at his squad. McGill steadied himself, fired and dropped a machine gunner. By his second shot, the machine gun turned its attention on him, forcing him to lay low. His squad took advantage of the distraction and forced the Germans back. McGill dropped another German on the run, making for his fifth hit for that patrol.

Among the 3rd Division's soldiers landing at Anzio was Platoon Sergeant E. L. Dean of Portland, Oregon. An expert shot, Dean used his sniper rifle to neutralize a machine gun that was annoying his platoon. He crawled out to within 900 yards of the gun and after adjusting his scope, waited. When the gun barked Dean fired and silenced it and followed it up with a second shot. On the next patrol the machine gun was gone. In another incident Dean hit a running German at 800 yards. Dean was modest about it, claiming it was a scratch shot but skill was certainly involved.

In Normandy, Private First Class Ray Register was scanning the line with binoculars when he sighted a machine gun being set up at the intersection of two hedgerows. Working the bolt on his scoped Springfield as fast as he could, he dropped all four

M1903A4 Springfield with M73B1 scope. (Springfield Armory National Historic Site)

Germans. His firing drew the attention of someone and Register noticed some movement in the hedgerow. An artillery observer had joined Register by now and Register asked him to spot. Steadying himself, Register fired one shot, heard a cry and didn't need a spotter—the German fell from the hedgerow.

Fighting in the Pacific alongside the Marines on Guadalcanal was Army Lieutenant John George. A competitive shooter, George brought a Springfield customized with a Lyman Alaskan scope on a Griffin & Howe scope mount:

> In a moment, I saw something a few yards away from the body that made me drop the glasses and grab for the rifle. A live Jap had just risen from beside the corpse. Stunned and deafened by the blast that had thrown him from the bunker, he was holding his head with both hands in what could well have been a comical expression of exasperation. He remained exposed, probably in great pain—perhaps with burst ear drums. With Art giving me frantic directions in a nervous stage whisper, I held the shot. The scope had a tapered, flat top post reticle, with a lateral cross hair, sighted in to strike center on a 10-inch bull with a six o'clock hold at 200 yards. As I took up the slack and aimed, the Jap was on his knees in a prayer-like attitude which was far more appropriate than he realized. … I nudged his chin with the broad post—a measure calculated to plant the bullet somewhere on his chest at the 350 yard range. Then I gave the least pound or so of the three pound trigger pull a "gentle snatch." The scope settled back in time for me to see the bullet strike the Jap and splash sand behind him.

While serving with Merrill's Marauders, George carried a M-1 carbine but always used his Springfield to snipe.

Within the Marine Corps, impetus for newer scoped rifles came in 1940 when Colonel Julian C. Smith recommended for consideration to the Commandant the Lyman Alaskan, Noske (2.5–4×), and Weaver 330 and 440 (2.5–4× respectively). No action was taken until July 19, 1942 when the Division of Plans and Policies wrote the Commandant: "It is believed that sniper training should be initiated in the Marine Corps in the near future;

that a suitable course be tentatively adopted for this purpose; and that after adoption of such course, sniper schools should be established." It also pointed out that the snipers' course developed by Major Van Orden was available on file at the Weapons School at Quantico and that an outline of a British snipers' course was available too. The Commandant was receptive and schools were set up on both the East and West Coast.

The West Coast school at Camp Elliot, San Diego, accepted the fifteen expert riflemen from each replacement battalion. The course was five weeks long and the top five graduates were sent to the Raiders for an additional three weeks of training. Course material included camouflage, concealment, spider traps, map and compass reading, use of the telescopic sight, scouting and patrolling, etc. Upon graduation, the men were distributed three per company but as specialists, were not attached to any platoon. The East Coast school at New River, North Carolina had twenty students per class for its three-week course.

Bronx native Bob Stiles enlisted after Pearl Harbor. Qualifying as expert at boot camp, he was asked to and became a scout-sniper. On Guadalcanal Stiles was summoned by his battalion commander, Lieutenant Colonel McKelvy, who told him that a company was pinned down by a sniper. Stiles described what happened next:

> So I moved over to where the company was and started moving through that damn konai grass and looking into the treetops. I was completely concealed by the konai yet I had a perfect view of those high trees. Eventually I saw some movement in one of the trees. Pretty soon a head and then a rifle barrel came into view. I had my rifle sling nice and tight and my sight elevation was perfect. I let go and, wham, out of the trees comes the Nip.

Unimpressed by USMC snipers on Okinawa was Private Sterling Mace: "I had already seen one of those snipers operate, and all he did was clean his rifle, look through his scope for a few minutes, and then resume the rifle cleaning. Over and over, he would perform this noble task, never deviating from the script; then, when he felt he had sniped enough, he'd move to another spot in the rocks in case the rocks on the Jap side of the line spotting him spotting them." Mace's opinion would probably be different if he witnessed Private Daniel Webster Case, 1st Marines, knock out a Japanese machine gun at 1,200 yards distance. Case's captain later told him that several bodies were stacked around the gun.

Post World War II

World War II concluded and the nuclear age meant that an army could be destroyed by one bomb. With exception of the Soviet Union and the British Royal Marines, sniping was forgotten. After all, the bomb meant ground warfare was highly unlikely; that is, until Korea broke out and schools were restarted in response, only to close when the necessity was over.

In 1960, U.S.M.C. Captain Jim Land temporarily opened a sniping school in Hawaii. Material gathered by Land was later used by Captain Bob Russell, 3rd Division, to open an in-country school in Vietnam. Vietnam was heating up and 1st Division General Herman Nickerson, Jr. ordered Land to open a school for his division. Land arrived in Vietnam in 1966 and began gathering personnel and equipment. He drew 30-06 Winchester Model 70 rifles from supply and, using recreation funds, bought scopes from the PX. Land transferred from the MPs a graduate of his Hawaii school, Carlos Hathcock. Hathcock not only instructed but became one of the highest scoring snipers in Vietnam with 93 kills. There were others like Army Sergeant Aldebert Waldron who had amassed 113 kills, Chuck Mawhinney with 103 and Eric England with 98.

Post Vietnam, the pattern repeated itself with sniping again being forgotten by the United States. However, one dedicated group, the Army Marksmanship Unit thought it more than competitive match skill but also useful on the battlefield. In 1977 the U.S.M.C. established a permanent sniping school and the U.S. Army followed. After 9/11, snipers proved their worth in fighting terrorism. When the *Maersk Alabama* was captured by pirates and its skipper, Richard Phillips held hostage in 2009, U.S. Navy SEAL snipers aboard the U.S.S. *Bainbridge* killed the three terrorists who were on the lifeboat with Phillips and captured the fourth who was aboard the *Bainbridge* negotiating Phillips' release. New long-distance records were made and broken including: Staff Sergeant James Gilliland's 1,250-meter kill with his 7.62 mm Nato M-24 rifle in Iraq in 2005; Sergeant Nick Ranstad, 1-91st Airborne Cavalry, with 2,100 meters in Afghanistan in 2008; Corporal Rob Furlong, Princess Patricia's Light Infantry, with 2,430 meters in 2002; and Sergeant Craig Harrison of the Blues and Royals, 2,475-meter kill in 2009.

The perception of snipers and sniping has changed over time. In the flintlock musket era it was thought unfair to aim. Civil War soldiers felt sharpshooting was murder and many disliked sharpshooters including their own sharpshooters. Hesketh-Prichard was called a professional assassin. In Vietnam snipers were derisively called "Murder Incorporated" after the Chicago gangland killers. Today, snipers enjoy the support of their fellow soldiers and officers as well as the public. As a force multiplier, they are seen as a necessary component that saves lives and prevents greater harm.

SELECT BIBLIOGRAPHY

Bailey, DeWitt, *British Military Flintlock Rifles 1740–1840* (Andrew Mowbray Pub., 2002)

Beaufoy, Henry [A Corporal of Riflemen, pseudo.], *Scloppetaria* (1808), (Richmond Publishing Co., 1971)

Bilby, Joseph, *Civil War Firearms: Their Historical Background and Tactical Use* (Da Capo, 1996)

Canfield, Bruce, *U.S. Military Bolt Action Rifles* (Andrew Mowbray Pub., 2010)

Canfield, Bruce, *U.S. Infantry Weapons of World War II* (Andrew Mowbray Pub., 1994)

Costello, Edward, *The True Story of a Peninsular War Rifleman* (Shinglepicker, 1997)

Crum, Frederick Maurice, *With Riflemen, Scouts, and Snipers, From 1914 to 1919* (Oxford, 1921)

Dunlop, William S., *Lee's Sharpshooters or The Forefront of Battle* (Morningside Bookshop, 1988)

Edward, William, *Civil War Guns* (Stackpole Company, 1962)

Flatnes, Øyvind, *From Musket to Metallic Cartridge* (Crowood Press, 2013)

Hesketh-Prichard, Hesketh, *Sniping in France: With Notes on Scientific Training of Scouts, Observers, and Snipers* (Langer Militaria, 1993)

Kincaid, John, *Random Shots From a Rifleman* (Spellmount, 1998)

LaCrosse, Richard B., *The Frontier Rifleman* (Pioneer Press, 2013)

Leach, Johnathan, *Rough Sketches From the Life of a Soldier* (Ken Trotman, 1986)

McBride, Herbert, *A Rifleman Went to War* (Lancer Militaria, 1987)

Pegler, Martin, *Out of Nowhere: A History of the Military Sniper* (Osprey Publishing, 2004)

Pegler, Martin, *Sniping in the Great War* (Pen & Sword Military, 2008)

Senich, Peter, *Complete Book of US Sniping* (Paladin Press, 1988)

Senich, Peter, *The German Sniper 1914–1945* (Paladin Press, 1982)

Senich, Peter, *United States Marine Corps Scout–Sniper* (Paladin Press, 1993)

Shore, Clifford, *With British Snipers to the Reich* (Lancer Militaria, 1988)

Skennerton, Ian, *The British Sniper* (Skennerton, 1983)

Stevens, Charles, *Berdan's United States Sharp Shooters in the Army of the Potomac* (Morningside Bookshop, 1984)

White, Russell C., *The Civil War Diary of Wyman White* (Butternut and Blue, 1993)

Yee, Gary, *Sharpshooters (1750–1900): The Men, Their Guns, Their Story* (Sharpshooter Press, 2009)

ACKNOWLEDGEMENTS

A book is a collaborative effort and this one is no exception. The author gratefully acknowledges the assistance of my readers including Lynn Baker, June Norman, Elias Santiago and Charlie Snow. Notable authors and researchers who assisted include: Joe Bilby, Bruce Canfield, Robert Cooper, Lawrence Babits of Eastern Carolina University, and Martin Pegler. Images for this work were provided by: Gettysburg National Military Park Curator Greg R. Goodell, 45th Infantry Division "Thunderbirds" Museum Director Michael Gonzalez, Springfield Armory National Historic Site Curator Alexander MacKenzie, West Point Military Museum Director Les Jenson, Mandi Ratchford, Jack Rouse, Michael Tahirak, Beth Newman and Ben van Hooser of Greenburg, Kentucky, and Trinidad State Junior College's Public Information Officer Greg Boyce. My mother Ann Yee photoshopped some images and my nephew, Zachary Killmaire assisted Greg Boyce. Another Trinidad State Junior College staffer who helped was Donna Haddow. I'd also like to thank the staff of Casemate Publishing and Ruth Sheppard in particular for making this book possible.

Finally any mistake and oversight in this work is mine alone for which I accept responsibility.